Praise
Through the Lens

"Allyson Apsey has a gift for storytelling. Through her stories, you learn about yourself and others in ways that you weren't expecting. Her stories are relatable in that you feel yourself in them even if you aren't a character. You feel compassion for the people Allyson has compassion for. You feel frustration for the tension in their lives. While trauma may be lurking behind each story, the real focus of this book is the people who are who they are because of the trauma they have experienced. And guess what? Whether we have experienced trauma or not, focusing on people first and foremost is the best thing we can do in any situation. Allyson brings that point home again and again throughout the book and inspires you to do the same."

—Jethro Jones, transformative principal

"Through the Lens of Serendipity is an eclectic blend of inspiration, research, and practical strategies that will help you be a more caring and consistent version of your best self. Allyson Apsey uses stories and a plethora of practical strategies empowering readers to get a handle on hope. The secret to living a truly happy life and helping others do the same has never been closer!"

—Brad Gustafson, national distinguished principal
and author of *Reclaiming Our Calling*

"Allyson emphasizes the importance of taking care of ourselves so that we can better understand and serve others. She encourages to see past our surface level interactions and see deep into each individual we encounter and find ways to help them grow in a side-by-side journey. If you are looking for a book that will make you and those around you better and make the world a better place, this is a great read."

—George Couros, author of *Innovator's Mindset*

"In her latest book, *Through the Lens of Serendipity*, Allyson Apsey shines a light on some of the courageous and empathetic ways we can support and uplift one another in school situations, at home, and even in an office environment. Apsey uses the power of story, personal examples, research, and fun anecdotes which made her first book, *The Path to Serendipity,* so memorable. If you are looking for strategies to support students or colleagues experiencing trauma in varying degrees, you will surely benefit from this book."

—Jennifer Casa-Todd, teacher-librarian and
author of *Social LEADia*

"*Through the Lens of Serendipity* continues the passionate 'from the heart' approach to education and life that Allyson Apsey started in *The Path to Serendipity*. In her latest book, Allyson shows us how to 'HANDLE' life situations in a positive and healthy manner by giving us the tools to help ourselves and others. Using a 'peopled-centered lens,' she guides us through specific steps to help us support those impacted by trauma, keep problems small, and avoid personalizing anger. If you're looking for ways to help support your school team, your family, or even yourself, then this book is what you are looking for!"

—Jonathon Wennstrom, Michigan principal

"'*Hope is everything: Even the tiniest spark of hope can help us work through challenges. When we lose hope, the same challenges can seem insurmountable.'*

"We all have challenges that we encounter. They can range from career to financial and everything in-between. *Through The Lens of Serendipity* is a wonderful and delightful book that is sure to increase your ability to reflect and grow along your own personal journey. Allyson shows true vulnerability by sharing real, heartfelt stories that have shaped her own life. Furthermore, this book will have you intentionally pausing and building empathy for people you see every single day."

—Ben Gilpin, Warner Elementary principal,
Western School District, Michigan

"*Through the Lens of Serendipity* is an offering to our world. It offers us the gift of growth, reflection, learning, love, and connection. Allyson's authentic voice and storytelling invite us to embrace our goodness and provide guidance to embrace, see, hear and feel the goodness of others. The greatest gift is that she offers us a way to support others in seeing and accepting the goodness within themselves. Don't just buy this book—read it. Use it. Live it. Offer it as a gift to others."

—**Marisol Rerucha,** educational leader, advocate and writer

"*Through the Lens of Serendipity* offers a master class in advanced empathy, while readers enjoy a beautiful journey into self dis-covery and personal development. Apsey *brilliantly* weaves the-ory with practice, without losing any of the whimsy, humor, and charm that made *The Path to Serendipity* such an outstanding suc-cess! This is simply PHENOMENAL educational literature! The heartfelt inspiring stories, learnings, and strategies have equally exceptional LIFE-CHANGING application inside and outside the school house. Indeed, anyone whose life has invariably inter-sected with another human being will undoubtedly find mean-ingful perspective to assist in one's current personal and pro-fessional relationships. *Through the Lens of Serendipity* provides a DELIGHTFUL roadmap to create a more fully actualized and healthy loving culture within our own circle of influence. Highest recommendation possible!"

—**Hans Appel,** middle school counselor and
creator of Award Winning Culture

"*Through the Lens of Serendipity* offers critical content related to trauma research, covering essential information and skills to respond well to those around us who have experienced trauma. As a real gift for readers, Allyson's signature engaging writing style weaves stories that provide the perfect lens for how we can HANDLE all people well. A great resource for reflection, research, theory, and practice!"

—**Sarah Johnson,** coauthor *Balance Like a Pirate*,
founder In AWE, LLC and host of In AWE Podcast

"As I read *Through the Lens of Serendipity*, I spent many days reading, rereading, and reflecting upon Allyson's words. I repeatedly read the chapters over and over to let Allyson's thought-provoking research and ideas simmer and sink in to a deeper level. There were many stories I could relate to. I love how Allyson brought my thinking to a whole new level. Allyson's words truly made me feel like a better person. This book has empowered me to tune into those around me and consciously maintain an open mind and open heart.

—**Karen Festa,** loving wife, mom of two amazing little girls, and passionate special educator who strives to inspire adults and children to shine a positive light and share goodness from within

"First, she astounded us with her authenticity in *The Path to Serendipity*, then she gave us *The Princes of Serendip,* an exceptional picture book for social-emotional learning. Allyson Apsey amazes yet again with this timely masterpiece on trauma-informed practices. She shares actionable, practical ways to show compassion and empathy to everyone around us. Whether in education or in any other career field, this book gives readers the tools needed to understand how to HANDLE others with care. *Through the Lens of Serendipity* should be on every bookshelf, highlighted and tabbed, to be referenced again and again."

—**Alicia Ray** (@iluveducating), lead digital learning and media innovation facilitator, mom, lifelong lover of learning, creator of #DBC50Summer and #DBCBookBlogs

Allyson once again uses her innate ability to connect with people through her relatable examples of how we can add value to others when we apply a people-centered approach. Her thought-provoking stories and lessons are not only applicable to the classroom setting and education arena, but they are also equally applicable in the boardroom, on the shop floor, and in any course of business that involves people. Adopting Allyson's positive attitude and applying her simple methods will lead to better results and more productive relationships in both your professional and personal lives.

—**Todd Wisner,** North American industrial manager (and Allyson's brother)

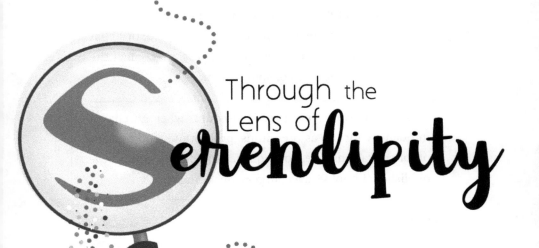

Through the
Lens of
Serendipity

Even if Life has Shown Them Its Worst

Helping Others
Discover the Best
in Themselves

Allyson Apsey

Enjoy
the
journey!

♡, Allyson
Apsey

Through the Lens of Serendipity
© 2019 by Allyson Apsey

This book is available at special discounts when purchased in quantity for use as premiums, promotions, fundraisers, or for educational use. For inquiries and details, contact the publisher at books@daveburgessconsulting.com.

Published by Dave Burgess Consulting, Inc.
San Diego, CA
DaveBurgessConsulting.com

Cover Design by Genesis Kohler
Editing and Interior Design by My Writers' Connection
Picture of author taken by Samantha Kraker, samanthakraker.com

Library of Congress Control Number: 2019931207
Paperback ISBN: 978-1-949595-22-2
Ebook ISBN: 978-1-949595-23-9

First Printing: May 2019

Dedication

For my sons, Laine and Tyson.

"Sons are the anchor of a mother's life."
—Sophocles

Contents

Foreword

by Deborah K. Heisz

CEO, cofounder, and editorial director,
*Live Happy **magazine***

What is it that makes the difference between a happy life and an unhappy one? I've spent the past several years studying what it takes to achieve real, sustainable happiness. What I've learned from all the research studies and real-life stories of happy people is that happiness isn't simply the result of an "easy" life.

For one thing, life isn't easy for anyone; we all face challenges and hardships to varying degrees. It's a reality that life isn't always kind; for some people, it seems particularly cruel. Abuse, physical or emotional abandonment, loss, homelessness, and hunger bring hardship without regard to age. So many people—far too many of them children—suffer the consequences of circumstances completely beyond their control. Even so, I'm sure you know people who have incredible stories of triumph after tragedy. They've endured unimaginable pain or struggles and refused to let life get them down. They've pushed forward to create a joyful life that is rich in relationships. Those people inspire us with their tenacity and grace under pressure. And they are genuinely happy.

You also probably know at least a few people for whom unhappiness, negativity, and fear are the norm. Their response to the very real challenges and hurts they've experienced is to lash out at perceived threats or withdraw completely into a protective shell. Relationships with those people can be difficult because mistrust is their "go-to" response. As a result, their behavior pushes people away—and a cycle of hurt, loneliness, and unhappiness persists.

What this contrast of behavior and experience teaches us is that the difference between people who are happy and those who aren't is not merely circumstance. Without question, our experiences have an impact on who we are. But it is also true *that the way we respond to life's challenges* and *how we* choose *to view the world* shapes who we become. These two traits very often determine whether we are happy.

The words that happiness researchers use to describe these elemental characteristics of happiness are *resiliency* and *positive attitude*. Resiliency is the ability and willingness to get up after you've been knocked down. We see it in people who refuse to quit after failure and in those who dare to try and to trust again. Resilient people persist because they believe they have a chance at success—a belief supported by a positive attitude that chooses to focus on possibilities rather than to dwell on hurt or shame. People who exhibit a positive attitude intentionally look for the good even in the worst circumstances. You could even say they view the world *through the lens of serendipity.*

Here's the good news: Resiliency and a positive mindset can be developed and strengthened like a muscle. You can practice intentionally by focusing your thoughts on possibilities rather than on doubts and fears. You can choose to take responsibility for the next moment no matter what happened to you yesterday, last month, or even what happened to you as a child. Happiness is a choice you can make for yourself.

Here's the even better news: By modeling resiliency and a positive attitude, you can help others develop those traits within themselves. No one can *make* another person happy—happiness is an inside job. But you can inspire others to practice the characteristics that lead to happiness by leading the way with hope, kindness, and grace when life doesn't go as planned.

In this book, Allyson Apsey asks us to focus on helping others see the potential for happiness in their lives. With a heart for those who are hurting, she shares insights that help us identify when people need to be handled with care. Sometimes that need stems from emotions brought on by trauma—be it recent or years ago. Sometimes people are just having a bad day. Regardless, as Allyson points out, we don't need to know everyone's history or circumstances to help them. We simply need to treat people with care—even (and perhaps especially) when their behavior doesn't make it easy.

Resiliency and a positive attitude can be learned—and they are best taught by example. Each time we reach out to help people up when life has knocked them down, we help them see they *can* get back up. And over time, we just may be able to help people discover the potential we see in them. Even better, we may inspire them to make choices that lead to a happier life.

Preface

What an incredible journey this authoring thing is. I have been blessed to connect with so many people who are out there working hard to live their best life and are helping other people to do the same. Beyond the joy of hearing from readers, I simply love to write. I get up at the break of dawn on weekends so that I can write. I am smiling really big right now as I type these words because I am so excited to spend a few quiet hours writing to you. And knowing that you are reading this is a huge gift to me because what I write is not about me. When you are reading this book, it is about you. Your journey, your experiences, your values, your connections. Thank you from the bottom of my heart for sharing some of you with me as you read this book.

The feedback I have received from readers of *The Path to Serendipity*, my first book and a prequel of sorts to *Through the Lens of Serendipity*, has been beyond my wildest dreams. When I read that people feel like *The Path to Serendipity* has changed their lives, I feel honored and humbled. I know that I am imperfect, but just like you, I'm working hard to be the best I can be for myself and for the people around me; I'm plagued with self-doubt at times, and I feel nervous about sharing what's on my heart. Like you, I feel a full range of emotions, including sadness, anger, and stress, but I am choosing joy and happiness as my constant state. Feelings (both those that make us feel great and those that leave us feeling lousy) are unavoidable and are necessary to living our best lives. They teach us empathy and gratitude and provide opportunities to strengthen our resolve.

Similar to *The Path to Serendipity,* this book is intended to take you on an emotional journey. My hope is that you will reflect on your own experiences and relationships and set goals for yourself. With that in mind, I've included a variety of stories that highlight different types of relationships so you can see how the lens of serendipity can be used to view every relationship in your life.

This book is different from *The Path to Serendipity,* which focuses on looking inward as we seek to learn how to become the best version of ourselves. *Through the Lens of Serendipity* offers a look around us, at the people we encounter every day—whether a casual acquaintance, or a family member, a colleague, or lifelong friend. We'll look at how we can best support the people around us, taking into account their background, experiences, and which challenges they face. One of my greatest passions in life is to support others so that they are able to be the best versions of themselves, and, at the very least, not make their lives more difficult. My background in Choice Theory training and my recent trauma-informed training has made me even more determined to support and empower everyone around me. We never know the challenges they are going through, and some of those experiences and challenges may well include trauma, which can have a significant impact on a person's life. One outcome I hope to achieve with this book is to help you develop the understanding that being trauma-informed is actually being compassionate to all people. The supports and strategies that are helpful to those who have experienced trauma are supports and strategies that benefit every single person.

Looking through the lens of serendipity means understanding that we all want good things in our lives, that we need to HANDLE each other with care, and that we will never know what the people we encounter have experienced in their lives.

I want to thank you again for being on this journey with me. I am stronger with you by my side. As you read, please share your connections, learning, and thoughts with all of us at #SerendipityEDU.

Love always,

Allyson

An Invitation

Do you ever feel like you're living behind the eight ball? Yeah, me too, all the time. In September 2017, I attended a presentation about becoming a trauma-informed educator. That is when I first learned about the ACEs study conducted by the Center for Disease Control and Intervention. The study happened at Kaiser-Permanante from 1995 to 1997, which was before I even became an educator, and there I sat, learning about it twenty years into my tenure. I felt fortunate to be armed with the knowledge and strategies I learned that day, and at the same time, I felt an incredible sense of urgency rushed over me. I suddenly realize that, for twenty years, I had missed out on opportunities to better serve the people in my path who have been affected by trauma. I did not want to waste another single second or miss another opportunity.

ACEs stands for "Adverse Childhood Experiences", and the study itself has become more widely known because of documentaries like *Resilience* (2016) and *Paper Tigers* (2015), both of which I highly recommend. Through the results of the study, we now know the significant impact childhood trauma has on children both emotionally and physically:

- Childhood trauma has a long-lasting impact. Through the ACEs study, childhood trauma has been linked to many of the leading causes of adult disease and death.

- Children who have experienced trauma have increased risk for obesity, risky behaviors, diabetes, heart disease, alcoholism, adolescent pregnancy, poor grades, and more.
- There is a dose-response correlation, meaning that the higher the exposure to trauma, the higher the risk of the health issues listed above.

We also know that trauma changes the brain as well as the body. We can no longer simply wish these adverse consequences of trauma away. We have to do something. Now.

> We can no longer simply wish these adverse consequences of trauma away.

I have always had a passion for equipping and encouraging people to take good care of themselves mentally and physically. I believe that when we are healthy and strong, it puts us in a position to be compassionate toward everyone around us. And everyone needs that compassion. Do a mental inventory of all the people you have encountered over the past few days. Visualize their faces. Now, know that for every ten faces you pictured, six of them have experienced some sort of adverse childhood trauma, be it verbal, physical, or sexual abuse, neglect, or witnessing abuse between parents. Before you tell me that you do not have time to get to know the history of everyone you meet, let me tell you that *you don't have to.* The reality is that we cannot get to know everyone we interact with on a daily basis on a deep or personal level. Some people have faced serious trauma and the rest are likely dealing with stress, insecurities, or heartache right now. So, yes, *everyone* needs your compassion.

We will never know some people's history or whether trauma has impacted their lives. So instead of trying to figure out everyone's past and how it might be affecting their present, let's just assume that all people want good things for themselves, that everyone has experienced hurt, loss, or challenges in some way, and that we are on this planet to help others—and to never hurt anyone. I wrote this book with the intention of helping you understand how past experiences and present motivations affect the way we all behave. Because I have a heart for helping those who have experienced trauma to thrive, we'll look at how we can all be better "trauma-informed." But the practices and strategies you'll find throughout this book aren't relegated to those with a history of trauma, violence, poverty, or other challenges. They apply to *all* of us.

I invite you to join me in looking at the world and the people around you through a compassionate, people-centered lens.

In this book, we will learn how understanding the motivation behind behavior—others' and our own—helps us relate to people and address their needs. In my first book, I explored Dr. William Glasser's five basic needs that drive all behavior. In this book, the focus is on how to understand your personal needs so you can be your best self and therefore more effectively help others.

As we look through the lens of serendipity together, we'll learn a few things:

- Know that there is always more to someone's story than what meets the eye.
- Review (or learn about) Glasser's five basic needs and expand on that learning by understanding how to change how we are thinking and feeling.

- Understand that looking for the good in all people benefits more than just the people around you—it benefits you as well.
- Begin to understand how our brains work and why someone might choose fight, flight, or freeze over pausing and problem-solving.
- Understand what trauma is and that the same compassion and supports that those who have been affected by trauma need benefit *all* people.
- Know that others' past experiences change their view on the world, their perceptions of others, and motivate their own self-preserving behaviors. And our own past experiences change our view of the world.
- Understand that we impact each other with our behavior, and this impact can be negative or positive.
- Passionately believe that in order to support everyone, we have to HANDLE each other with care.

Hope is everything.

Assure safety.

no shoulda' needed.

Do things differently.

Listen to understand.

Establish trust.

This beautiful life we live offers us a kaleidoscope of feelings and emotions. The gorgeous rainbow painted by all of our experiences is full of incredible highs and gut-wrenching lows. If we can be of help to each other on the journey, we feel like we can face just about any-thing. Together we are so very strong.

Together we are
so very strong.

Chapter 1

The Secrets Our Smiles Contain

The real man smiles in trouble, gathers strength from distress, and grows brave by reflection.

—Thomas Paine

Allie walked down the street as if she didn't have a care in the world. Her brown hair was blowing in the breeze, and her long, stylish pants exposed just a peek of her designer heels. The little knowing smile she wore told a story of its own. It was as if she had a special secret and was fooling the world by keeping the information to herself. She did, in fact, have a secret. A lot of them, actually. But no one would ever guess the secrets her smile contained.

• • •

Not too many years ago, if I had passed Allie on the street, I would have smiled at her, all the while desperately wishing I looked like her with those long legs and all that obvious confidence. I would have guessed that she lived in a luxurious condo downtown with daily housekeeping and an indoor parking spot for her fancy car. I would have assumed that she had a husband who adored her and would do anything for her, someone who smiled as he brought her coffee in bed every morning. In short, I would have assumed that Allie's life was perfectly perfect.

And I would have been wrong. No one's life is perfect. "Perfect" just doesn't exist. Let's go back to Allie's story to see what lay behind that secretive smile.

"Perfect" just doesn't exist.

Okay, I can do this. Allie thought to herself. *I was a hot mess yesterday when I walked away from the party, but I am not going to let that define my day. Today is a bright new day, and I am going to conquer my fears.*

Allie's mind went back to the monthly office birthday party that took place at the end of the workday yesterday. Her stomach sank again remembering the moment when she walked into the conference room and saw her colleagues divided into groups of friends—none of which she fit into. Everyone was already at the party when she arrived, and it felt as if she were back at the high school dance. Groups of three or four were huddled in the corners, talking and laughing as they ate their cake. Not a single person glanced at Allie as she went over to the cake table. She walked away without grabbing a piece because her stomach was in knots.

Allie overheard bits of the conversation happening in one corner of the room. Three of the women who work in her department (the three who seem to hate her the most) were giggling about something.

Allie's ears perked when she heard her name. Honing in on that conversation, she heard bits and pieces.

"She won't even eat the cake. She thinks she is too good for our mere mortal food."

"What is her problem? She walks around like she is the queen of the office, but she never talks to us."

"I bet she will get that promotion. She gets everything she wants."

If they only knew. If they only asked. She would tell them. Maybe she should march over there right now and tell them what her life is really like, why she is so quiet and why their gossip felt like acid poured onto a raw wound. Allie took a step in their direction. And then promptly stepped right back, turned around, and walked out of the room.

Allie's childhood had been hard before her brother left, but after he left, her life became unbearable. He was her protector, and without him, her family crumbled into dysfunction. Her mom had balanced three jobs her whole life, and although she loved her kids very much, she had nothing left for them when she finally got home from work. Allie and her brother had had to depend on themselves and on each other. Allie had learned how to make macaroni and cheese when she was four years old.

Allie's dad left before she was born. Her brother could still remember him and had memories of a time when they were all happy and did family things that Allie had only ever read about in books. They went to the park, took weekend getaways, and had Sunday meals with extended family. Allie loved hearing those stories, loved thinking that there was once normalcy in their family. It gave her hope for her own future.

Her brother had tried to create some of those experiences for Allie by doing things like taking her to the nearby playground and teaching her how to play basketball. Those were some of the best memories from her childhood. That, and school. School had been an escape for Allie. She felt normal there. Better than normal, actually, because she could excel at school. School hadn't come easy for Allie, but she quickly learned that by trying hard she earned her teachers' attention, and she thrived on their praise.

Allie was in eighth grade when her brother went away. She still doesn't know the full story because he won't talk about it with her, but she had learned some of it through the local news. Her brother and a few friends broke into a house and one of her brother's friends had a gun. She knew that her brother had nothing to do with that part. He couldn't have anything to do with the gun. Her brother's friend drew the gun on the homeowner when he unexpectedly came home in the middle of the robbery.

Allie's mom had been no help during the whole ordeal. She was barely able to function in their day-to-day life, but the situation with her brother had pushed her over the edge. There were many nights that Allie's mom had just cried and rocked on the couch for hours. She wouldn't talk to Allie for days. That was when Allie began to withdraw from the world. She understood that she was all alone, and that if she didn't want to get hurt again, she needed to shut out the world and rely only on herself.

Allie dug in and worked even harder in school after that. She graduated as class valedictorian and went on to attend her local college with a full scholarship. Two years ago she got this great job and has been working her way up the ranks in her company. Lately, though, her insecurities had started getting the best of her. Once again, fear of rejection and hurt enticed her to withdraw from others. She knew that it wasn't good for her, but old habits die hard. And the glares and gossip of the cliques around the office were not helping. At all.

● ● ●

I wonder if Allie's colleagues would they treat her differently if they knew her story. Man, I hope so. If not, all hope might be lost for them. It is unfortunate that people like Allie who have experienced trauma in their lives often experience additional trauma because of people like the colleagues in Allie's office. Misunderstandings and assumptions continue a spiral of negativity and hurt. The question is, how can we stop this cycle? How can we instead support one another to live hopeful and effective lives where we feel a deep sense of belonging on a daily basis? I wonder if there's someone in your life whose behavior irritates or even hurts you? Could there be something going on in his or her life that is causing or has led to that behavior? If you knew that person's story, would you treat them differently? My guess is that if you were to look at everyone you meet with compassion, their behavior and your own would significantly change.

> *Everyone you meet is fighting a battle you know nothing about. Be kind. Always.*
>
> —Brad Meltzer

In this book, we will explore many stories like Allie's as we reflect on our own relationships and behavior. No one's life is perfect. It's time to stop pretending that perfection exists—to stop *seeking* perfection. And it's most definitely time to stop hurting others in our pursuit of the unobtainable. Instead, let's start looking at everyone we encounter with kindness and lift up those people by acknowledging the good that is within them.

I am with you on this journey to becoming a more compassionate, people-centered person, knowing that this journey benefits me just as much as it benefits all the people I encounter.

Serendipitous Lessons

- Perfection will always elude us, no matter how much we seek it. It does not exist. So many of just want to feel normal, to feel like we are enough.
- We are all looking for the same good things in life.
- We may never know the truth behind that little knowing smile we see.
- We have a responsibility to help each other, and no right to hurt one another.
- Life is hard enough without us pouring acid on open wounds.

#SerendipityEDU

Which connections did you make to Allie's story? What assumptions have you made about others in the past that you are now rethinking? What is your first step to becoming more compassionate?

Share your story at #SerendipityEDU

Through a People-Centered Lens

We all travel different paths,
Each journey unique.

The experiences we have,
The values of the people we love

Are etched on our hearts
And in our minds.

My lens on the world is unique
To me and is mine alone.

Your lens is just as special as mine.

A people-centered lens is knowing that

Although our perceptions
May be worlds apart,

We can come together in
Mutual understanding

Of the good things we all seek.

Because, really, in the end,

We all seek the same things.

Chapter 2

Change Yourself and the World Changes

We but mirror the world . . . . If we could change ourselves, the tendencies in the world would also change. As a man changes his own nature, so does the attitude of the world change towards him . . . We need not wait to see what others do.

—Mahatma Gandhi

"Am I a different kind of principal?" I asked Sam, a fifth-grade boy who stood in my office.

He nodded vigorously.

"Is your teacher a different kind of teacher than the other teachers you've had?"

Again, Sam's head bobbled up and down.

"Okay then, if you want things to really be different at this school, there is one last thing that has to be different. You. Are you ready to be different?" I asked.

Sam's eyes widened with surprise at the question. Then he gulped and nodded slowly.

In order for things to change, *we* have to change. This is such a hard concept for children to understand because it seems unfair. Actually, come to think of it, this is a hard concept for adults to understand because it seems unfair. Much of the time, we refuse to consider that it is our fault that things are going badly. Right or wrong, we want to blame others for our troubles. Sometimes it is someone else's fault. But that doesn't matter because as Gandhi taught us, if we change ourselves, the world around us also changes.

> In order for things to change,
> we have to change.

For Sam, school had been a series of failures, not with learning but with relationships. He had been in trouble since he was in kindergarten. He had not been able to get along with fellow students or with teachers. Each year had repeated like a scene from that movie *Groundhog Day* with Bill Murray: Sam gets all dressed up in his new school clothes, throws on his crisp new backpack stuffed with all the glue sticks and pencils and markers a child could dream of on the first day of school, and walks into school hoping that this year will be different. Then *boom!* Again he is expected to know how to handle his anger with classmates when things don't go his way. He is expected to follow directions from teachers who seem just the same as the teachers from last year and the year before that and the year before that. And each year, his teachers acted as if they were surprised and disappointed when Sam behaved the same way that had gotten him in trouble every other school year.

Honestly, how could Sam, or *anyone*, have expected for things to be different when nothing but the page on the calendar had changed?

But things were different the year he came to my office for the first time. His teacher and I were not like those from his previous school experiences. We looked at Sam through a different lens, one not discolored by the past. And we gave him the encouragement and the opportunity to change.

In order for things to be different, we must be different.

I remember an encounter with another student, Beth. Before Beth entered our school, we found out about her previous difficulties with disrupting, refusing to work, and aggression, and we knew we had a golden opportunity to change the trajectory of her school career and maybe even her life. Beth's arrival came at the perfect time because our entire district was fortunate enough to hear Dr. Stephanie Grant, a developmental psychologist who focuses on infants and children with attachment concerns and trauma histories, talk about becoming trauma-informed educators. We didn't have to hear all the details about Beth's life to understand that she has experienced trauma that no adult, much less a little girl, knows how to handle.

The adults in our school understood that to help Beth have a different kind of school year, we had to be different. So we were. We put together a comprehensive plan that we reviewed regularly to make sure it was still providing the support she needed. We decided that we would make the school office a place where Beth could get her needs met. (Well, actually, in most schools, students often end up in

The adults in our school understood that to help Beth have a different kind of school year, we had to be different.

the office as they are working hard to get their needs met. Usually though, it is only after causing a problem in the classroom that the student is sent to the office for the one-on-one attention that he/she so desperately needs.)

We understood that Beth craved attention, and we were determined to make sure she wouldn't have to act out to get it. We built it into her schedule and gave her the opportunity to go to the office whenever she felt like she needed something. Beth had a teacher with a huge heart, lots of patience, and decades of teaching experience. Her teacher was willing to put aside "how things are usually done" and made a plan to help Beth get what she needed. Our two office secretaries, wonderfully patient women with many years of experience and expertise, were also willing think outside the box to meet Beth's needs. As her principal, I delighted in walking into the office to see our secretaries laughing with Beth when she visited. By meeting her needs *within* the functions of her school day, she no longer needed to act out to get the attention she craved. Here is the specific plan we used. It isn't rocket science; it's mostly borrowed from other really smart people, but it works very well.

Check in and Connect

Beth came to the office three times a day to check in and connect, for a total of about eight minutes a day. First, Beth came down to the office as soon as she put her coat and bag away. We asked her five simple questions, and it took as little as two to three minutes. To help her identify her feelings, we used a poster that shows faces expressing different emotions. I typically asked Beth the questions, sometimes helping her make goals based upon the behavior I saw from her and/ or input from her classroom teacher. If I was not in the office, one of our secretaries or even other teachers passing through the office asked her the questions. Sometimes Beth wrote the answers, and sometimes we did the writing for her. She came back for a quick check-in as she transitioned from lunch to recess. That check-in took only about one minute. Last, Beth checked in with us right before she went home. We quickly went over the goals she set for herself in the morning, and she let us know if she met those goals. This connection took about three to four minutes.

Water and Snacks

We had a little bottle of water in our office refrigerator labeled "Beth," and she was welcome to get it whenever she wanted it. She was always so careful to return it so it would be ready for her the next time. It didn't matter why she said she needed water—whether she was just thirsty, had a sore throat, if she wanted some attention, or if she needed a break from the classroom. We also kept healthy snacks in the office so she could come get a bite to eat anytime she needed it. If she forgot her snack or hadn't eaten enough for breakfast or lunch, she knew there was always something for her in the office. (Side note: Dr. Stephanie Grant suggests keeping carrot sticks in the office for students who are hungry. No one has ever binged on carrot sticks, right?)

Band-Aids/Ice/TLC

Whenever Beth came to the office, we gave her whatever she said she needed, be it a Band-Aid for an invisible paper cut, ice for a perceived bump on her knee, or a few minutes of time to just sit and read her book.

When talking with an experienced teacher who has attended many professional learning opportunities about becoming a trauma-informed educator, I asked her what the biggest takeaway has been from all her training. I will never forget her two-word response: "Believe them."

We believed Beth, and we *believed in* Beth. We didn't just tell her we believed in her. We demonstrated our belief by responding when she asked for help. Very quickly, she learned that all she had to do was ask for the help she needed. There were occasions when Beth needed redirection or had struggles, but she did not come to the office after acting out in class. The office was a very need-satisfying place for Beth, and if she figured out that all she had to do was disrupt the learning in the classroom to be sent there, she likely would be constantly disrupting the learning in the classroom. So we developed a different system to address disruptive or negative behavior.

"Believe them."

Everyone who encountered Beth on a daily basis agreed that the joy she brought to our lives far outweighed any investment in the time or support we provided her. The year was not without its ups and downs, but we were able to help Beth see herself as a successful student.

Being "different" really can be this simple. For Beth, check-ins, water and snacks, Band-Aids, ice, and TLC made a huge difference in the way she viewed and behaved in school. The biggest difference maker of all was that we believed her and that we believed in her. That's one of the best gifts you can give to any child.

Be the Change EVERY Day

One April day, I was plumb out of patience, and wouldn't you know it, Beth was too. I impatiently tried to get her to work out a problem with me so I could get back to one of the hundred other tasks I needed to accomplish. In response to my tension, she ran and hid under a table in the hallway. I was taken aback; I had not seen this behavior from her all year long. I mentally slapped myself upside the head, realizing that she had reverted to old behaviors because I had reverted to old behaviors. I was treating her with the same irritation and annoyance that she had experienced in school in years past. Of course she would run and hide. Who wouldn't?

I backtracked myself out of the corner I had painted us both into, and with the gift of some time to cool down, we worked it out. That encounter serves as a constant reminder that when we treat students the way they have always been treated, they will behave the way they have always behaved. Even after months of building trust that school was going to be different, one quick slip-up sent us several steps backward. Fortunately, I caught myself quickly and turned the situation around before too much damage was done to the trust in our relationship.

> When we treat students the way they have always been treated, they will behave the way they have always behaved.

The Same Ideas Apply to Any Workplace

These concepts and techniques don't just apply to students, educators, and school. Every workplace has employees who have experienced trauma and challenges in their lives. Like Beth, they need to be handled with compassion and understanding in order to help them do their very best work. If you lead a team of nurses, there is likely to be at least one nurse who needs more frequent check-ins in order to develop trusting relationships. If you are a department store manager, you may have never considered having carrot sticks available in the staff refrigerator, but why not? You likely have employees who regularly skip meals and come to work hungry (and cranky).

All of these strategies can be adjusted and applied to your setting because these needs for connection, trust, and care are universal to adults and children alike. Do you want to have an incredibly need-satisfying culture at your workplace? Do you want employees to *want* to do their very best work, take feedback willingly, and remain loyal to the company? Then embrace that you will have to do things differently for them if you want them to do things differently for you.

Everyone wants to be seen. We all want to be valued for the people we are and all the experiences we bring with us to the workplace. I'm sure that you want to be believed and hope others assume you have good intentions. If that's true for you, it's true for the people around you, too. Be the person who recognizes others' strengths. If you are a boss or leader, ensure that your employees have a need-satisfying work environment. That's how you get people to do their best work and secure their loyalty. Even when the work is hard, even when their personal lives are a mess, even if they are offered a more lucrative job somewhere else, your employees will want to stay if you create the right kind of culture. Be the boss who does things very differently, and you will be the boss who gets very different results from employees.

Everyone wants to be seen.

Remember Sam? He wanted school to be different, but candidly admitted, "I don't know how to do that."

Your teammates or staff members may be in the same position—wanting things to change, but uncertain as to *how* to change themselves. If that's the case, work together to outline some simple steps for change. We can never just stop doing something without replacing it with another behavior, which means that people need to know what to do—not just what *not* to do.

One of the big boulders in Sam's path to success was his angry, defensive reaction to being told to do something he didn't want to do. This ingrained pattern of behavior showed up even at seemingly silly and insignificant requests. We worked on small, simple steps to help him change his behavior. His initial goal was to say, "Okay," once per day. After he accomplished that, we moved on to other goals. Slowly Sam's guard came down and his relationships began to grow. Success builds upon success, no matter how small it is.

Success builds upon success,
no matter how small it is.

Serendipitous Lessons

- Changing ourselves changes the world around us.
- One of the best things you can do for a child is to believe them.
- Being different is not rocket science. Sometimes the simplest ideas can have the biggest impact.
- Creating a need-satisfying, supportive workplace or school helps others be their very best.
- We all run out of patience sometimes. When you do, throw it in reverse and back yourself out of that situation.

#SerendipityEDU

Regardless of our professions, we all experience situations where we would like to change in the way we respond to others. When you heard Sam's and Beth's stories, which experiences did you think about?

Share your story at #SerendipityEDU

Chapter 3
Living Our Most Effective Lives Comes First

God gave us the gift of life; it is up to us to give ourselves the gift of living well.

—Voltaire

I sometimes think that my teenage son speaks a totally different language than I do. There are times I will be convinced that he is so angry with me that I must have done something to mortally offend him, and I cannot for the life of me figure out what I did. I watch him move through his routines with a pensive look on his face, not making eye contact with me, and I wrack my brain to try to figure out what I did. I ask him if I did anything to upset him, and I don't believe him when he tells me no. Then I distract myself with something to buy a little time. Because we all know that time heals most wounds.

Later, when we have a few minutes alone to talk about the day a bit, I ask him again what was so upsetting to him. More often than not, it turns out that whatever it was had nothing to do with me. Not a thing. He may have been worried about a school assignment or a friend or he just woke up on the wrong side of the bed.

Sometimes the behavior we see in others doesn't give us a clue about what is going on inside them. At school, students say they are bored when they are really confused. Children push a classmate on the playground when what they really want is a friendship with that person. Such behavior is confusing when it happens with children, but it can be baffling when we see it in adults.

When I studied William Glasser's Choice Theory many years ago,

> Sometimes the behavior we see in others doesn't give us a clue about what is going on inside them.

I learned that all behavior is motivated by the goal of meeting one or more of our five basic needs. That single realization changed my life. If you read my first book, *The Path to Serendipity*, you know that learning about Glasser's five basic needs saved me during my first year of teaching.

Everyone is trying to meet his or her needs for freedom, power, belonging, fun, and survival—all the time. That means *all* behavior is purposeful, and we have to look beyond the surface to understand what the true motivation is for any behavior.

Dr. Glasser taught us that we all have five need tanks within us, one for each of the five basic needs. The tanks are all different sizes for every person, depending on the strength of each need.

Take a minute to apply this to yourself. Rank the strength of your needs on a scale from one to five, one being the lowest and five being the highest. You can use these questions as a guide, and you can use a number more than once.

Survival: Do you avoid taking physical risks? Is it important to you to have a significant amount of money in your savings account? If so, you may have a high need for survival. Instead, do you love to do things like skydive or swim with the sharks? Does money flow freely through you? If you answered yes to one or both of these questions, you may have a low need for survival.

Freedom: Is it important to you to have lots of choice throughout your day? Do you feel your best when you have freedom with your time? A yes answer to one or both of these questions may indicate a high need for freedom. Or are you okay with things being tightly scheduled for you? Are you comfortable with others making decisions for you? These are indicators of a low need for freedom.

Power: Do you like to be in charge? Is having influence over others important to you? Or does the idea of being responsible for others make you sweaty and nervous? If you really like to be in charge and have influence over others, you likely have a high need for power. If you'd rather let someone else take the reins, you likely have a lower need for power.

Belonging: When you have a few minutes to yourself, do you reach for your phone to connect with the people you love the most? Would you rather do something on your own or with other people? Do you determine the effectiveness of your life by how many strong relationships you have? If so, you likely have a high need for belonging. If you usually would rather be alone or if you don't really think about the number of strong relationships you have, you might have a lower need for belonging.

Fun: Is having fun important to you? Do you love to belly laugh? Do you dance while you do the dishes? Are you described as playful? If you try your best to make most things you do fun, even if you make a fool of yourself in the process, you may have a high need for fun. If you are more about getting the work done than having fun while doing it, you may have a lower need for fun.

How might understanding the strengths of your own needs help you live an effective life? How might that change how you look at yourself?

Understanding that all behavior is purposeful and that we are all trying to meet our own needs all the time helps us look at ourselves with a different lens. When I am frustrated, I can dig in and look for the motivation behind my behavior. What need am I trying to meet? If I am not able to meet that need in the way I am currently trying to, is there another way I could meet that need?

> Understanding that all behavior
> is purposeful helps us look at
> ourselves with a different lens.

I have a high need for fun. (You will find that I am a pretty needy gal—I have high needs for fun, power, and belonging. And survival and freedom aren't that far behind.) One of the times in my life where I am really out of sorts is when I am packing for my family for a trip—like, running around like a grumpy, crazy woman out of sorts. I have lots of experience packing for weekend getaways because we have often lived a few hours from family, so I should be good at it by now. I am not.

We know from brain research that when the brain is stressed, the animal "fight, flight, or freeze" reactions surface. That's true even when for simple stressors like packing for a trip. And it is a cycle: I get stressed out and am impatient with everyone, then *their* "fight, flight, or freeze" response revs up because they get stressed out by my stress. Then I get even more stressed out because they are impatient with me. Yikes! Now, if you or I experience this problem—even in simple and recurring situations like packing for a trip—just think about the stressors our kids experience every day and how their brains, which aren't yet fully developed, might react.

I have identified that most of my problems with packing are due to the tight timelines I function within day to day. I work all week. When I need to get ready for a weekend away, I have to do so quickly and usually end up doing it at the last minute. Therefore, I don't spend time thinking about how I could make packing more fun. And the orders I bark to my family sometimes (most of the time?) fall on deaf ears—which does not help me meet my high need for power. If I want packing to be a more enjoyable experience for me and for my family, I need to figure out a way to meet my high needs for fun and power while I pack. Maybe I could make a list for my boys with a timeframe for completion. Maybe I could put my headphones in and dance around to my favorite songs while I gather everything we need. Those two little changes could make packing a need-satisfying activity and therefore help me smile and dance through the chore rather than acting like a grumpy, frazzled woman.

Before we can effectively support the people around us, we need to support ourselves in living our best, most effective lives. If I stay in balance because I am doing a good job meeting my own needs, then I am much better able to help my family, friends, students, and colleagues understand how to live their best lives and meet their own needs. No one can meet another person's needs. I cannot meet my son's need for freedom. I can, however, help create an environment where he can easily meet his own needs, and he can do the same for me. Until we understand what each of us needs and how we are alike and different, we will have a hard time creating a need-satisfying environment.

I have studied Choice Theory for years, and I think I have a pretty good handle on what I need to live an effective life. I have also analyzed my family pretty thoroughly (maybe much to their dismay). Even with all that reflection, the first thing I do when my sons or husband seems upset is blame myself or look for what I did wrong. Humans in general are pretty egocentric, which means we often believe that things happening around us have *way* more to do with us than they actually do. When someone is upset and tells me that it has nothing to do with me, it probably has nothing to do with me. Understanding the motivation of our own behavior and the behavior of the people around us is a constant work in progress.

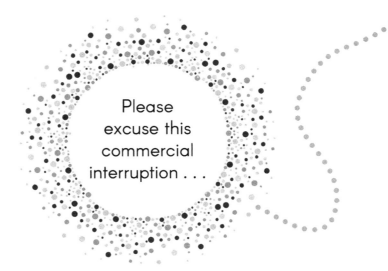

Please
excuse this
commercial
interruption . . .

Buy the Magic Mind-Reader Glasses TODAY!

Do you ever wish you could read someone's mind instead of wondering what they are thinking or why they seem angry? There's no need to wonder anymore! Get your very own pair of Magic Mind-Reader Glasses today! Don't delay!

With these special glasses, you can look at someone and instantly know whether they are upset with you or upset about something that has nothing to do with you. If the person is upset with you, your *Magic Mind-Reader Glasses* will turn a red tint. If it has nothing to do with you at all, the lenses will stay crystal clear.

The *Magic Mind-Reader Glasses* have been tested on hundreds of participants in a university study. They were accurate 100% of the time! The glasses stayed clear when the angry subjects were mad about something other than the person wearing the glasses. The red tint never appeared because the angry subjects were never angry with the person wearing the glasses, even when their behavior indicated something different.

Bonus! If you act now, you will get a second pair FREE, so a loved one can know that they are not the source of your anger either. *Bonus!*

Two for the price of one!

Just $9.99 plus S/H

Call 1-800-TheWorldDoesn'tRevolveAroundYou TODAY!

Serendipitous Lessons

- The purpose for a behavior may be hard to determine based upon what we see.
- All of our behavior is motivated by our five basic needs.
- We all have the same five basic needs, but the strength of these needs varies from person to person.
- Understanding what we need helps us live our most effective lives, and we have to do that before we can help others live their most effective lives.
- We cannot meet others' needs, but we can create an environment where they can easily meet their own needs.
- We cannot eliminate stress, but we can manage it to lessen the impact on us and the people we love.
- I am a pretty needy gal, and my packing skills (or lack thereof) need some major work.
- Like the "scientifically proven" Magic Mind-Reader Glasses reveal, other people's emotions usually have little to do with us.

#SerendipityEDU

Which of your needs do you find most difficult to meet? What new understanding did you develop about yourself and/or about a loved one?

Share your story at #SerendipityEDU

Chapter 4
Being Trauma-Informed Helps Everyone

The history of discovery is full of creative serendipity.

—Tom Kelley

A friend sent me the above quotation in a Christmas card, and as you can imagine, I love it. The beautiful thing about learning how to be a trauma-informed person is that, in doing so, you discover what it means to be a people-centered person. There is creative serendipity in discovering the happy accident that occurs when you become trauma-informed: you learn that it will benefit all the people in your life. The supports that allow people affected by trauma to heal and grow are good for all people. Focusing on having strong, positive relationships and being empathetic are the backbone of a trauma-informed approach to life and to life in general. Trauma sensitivity is people sensitivity.

In the next few chapters, we are going to turn our discovery into creative serendipity by looking at how we can HANDLE each other with great care. HANDLE is an acronym for . . .

Hope is everything: Even the tiniest spark of hope can help us work through challenges. When we lose hope, the same challenges can seem insurmountable.

Assure safety: If someone is worried about their physical safety, they cannot think about anything else. That means they cannot easily learn or regulate their emotions. Assuring safety helps calm fears and helps learning and problem-solving occurs.

no shoulda' needed: Raise your hand if a little kick of judgment from others helps you solve problems and feel better about yourself. Looking around, I don't see a single hand raised. As I learned from a very wise woman, it never helps to "should" all over people.

Do things differently: If we want things to be different, *we* have to be different. Not only because the only person we can control is ourselves, but also because we will never get different results by doing things the same way over and over.

Listen to understand: This is a passion of mine and something that has the power to solve some of our biggest problems. Really listening to gain an understanding of others' perceptions, values, and biases can help us work on solving problems with accurate information, which is so very helpful.

Establish trust: Trust takes concentrated effort to build and is fragile. After all that work to build it, it can still be broken in one seemingly small swoop. Mutual vulnerability requires trust, and strong, positive relationships require mutual vulnerability. This may come last in the acronym, but establishing trust has to come first in any relationship.

What Is Trauma?

Contrary to conventional thinking, trauma is not something that happens *to* you. It is something that happens *within* you as a result of an event or series of events. If we look at Allie's story from Chapter 1, we can easily identify many traumatic experiences she endured. The questions below helps us determine her ACEs score. This is an analysis of adverse childhood experiences, so the questions pertain specifically to experiences before the age of eighteen. There are ten questions and each yes counts as one, each no counts as zero, so everyone ends up with an ACEs score between 0 and 10.

1. Did a parent or other adult in the household often swear at you, insult you, put you down, or humiliate you? Act in a way that made you afraid that you might be physically hurt?
2. Did a parent or other adult in the household often push, grab, slap, or throw something at you? Ever hit you so hard that you had marks or were injured?
3. Did an adult or person at least five years older than you ever touch or fondle you or have you touch their body in a sexual way? Try to or actually have oral, anal, or vaginal sex with you?
4. Did you often feel that no one in your family loved you or thought you were important or special? Your family didn't look out for each other, feel close to each other, or support each other?
5. Did you often feel that you didn't have enough to eat, had to wear dirty clothes, and had no one to protect you? Your parents were too drunk or high to take care of you or take you to the doctor if you needed it?
6. Were your parents ever separated or divorced?

7. Was your mother or stepmother often pushed, grabbed, slapped, or did she have something thrown at her? Sometimes or often kicked, bitten, hit with a fist, or hit with something hard? Ever repeatedly hit or threatened with a gun or knife?

8. Did you live with anyone who was a problem drinker or alcoholic or who used street drugs?

9. Was a household member depressed or mentally ill, or did a household member attempt suicide?

10. Did a household member go to prison?

From the little that we know about Allie, we could guess that she has an ACEs score of at least five. We know that her parents were separated or divorced, and we know her brother went to prison. In addition, we can reasonably suspect that her mom was mentally ill or depressed, that there were times she felt that no one in her family loved her or thought she was special, and that she did not have enough to eat at times, wore dirty clothes, and had no one to protect her. We don't know if her mom was ever abused by a boyfriend, and we don't know if Allie suffered any kind of physical abuse, so her score could certainly be higher. With an ACEs score of five, Allie has a much greater chance than others to smoke, to engage in risky behaviors, to have a mental illness, or to even have serious illnesses like heart disease or cancer.

Allie does have a few positive things stacked in her favor, however. Not every adverse experience has to be traumatic. If a child has a buffer (aka a caring, loving, trusted adult), their circumstances may not feel traumatic to them. Dr. Bruce Perry, psychologist and childhood trauma researcher and expert, says this:

The quality of a child's relationships before, during, and after a horrible event influences outcomes tremendously. Children who have experienced attentive, loving parental care since birth and who live in stable, safe homes and communities will fare best. A child will also respond to an event based on how the adults around her respond. Human emotions are contagious. If a child falls down and scrapes a knee, she will mirror the parent's response to the accident. If the parent is calm, it strengthens the child's stress-response system. If the parent views the situation as threatening, the child will, too. Parents' reactions turn out to be one of the major predictors of whether a child will develop symptoms of post-traumatic stress after a tragedy. Resilient children are made, not born.

Not every adverse experience has to be traumatic.

It is possible that Allie's brother served as a shield to protect Allie from experiencing traumatic effects of their circumstances. Her brother may have provided enough stability to allow Allie to develop some resiliency. He was not there, however, to protect her from the impact of his imprisonment. Nor was he there to act as a buffer from her mother's emotional difficulties after her brother went to prison.

Allie's childhood experiences clearly affected her and continue to impact the way she interacts with others and perceives herself and those around her. Rather than hurting her by gossiping about her and excluding her, her coworkers could actually help her by asking the question: *What does Allie need from us to help her heal and recover from her adverse childhood experiences?* As someone who is seeking to be trauma-informed or even simply compassionate, you can ask that question regarding the people in your life. When we are interacting, does neutral exist? Does everything we do either help or hurt those around us? Every day, we have the opportunity to help people through simple acts of kindness and compassion. And, through the training I've received to become more trauma-informed, I believe it is our responsibility to help others when it is in our power to do so.

Our Prefrontal Cortex and Limbic System

We don't have to be neuropsychologists to understand some of the research around how trauma affects the brain. In very simple terms, there are two components to our brain: the thinking part of our brain called the prefrontal cortex, and the basic emotions part of our brain called the limbic system. Let's go back to Sam, that student who reacts defensively to seemingly benign comments. Sam may have experienced significant trauma earlier in his life, in which accusations of wrongdoing led to yelling or even violence. The fear brought on by that kind of experience could cause his limbic system to jump into action even when Sam was given gentle directions or correction. In other words, Sam's limbic system threw him into a fight response to help protect him. Before his prefrontal cortex had time to think through what was being asked of him, his lightning-fast limbic system simply reacted.

Our first effort to help Sam better control his behavior was to tell him to "think before you act," but the phrase had no effect. What *did* work was helping him understand how his brain worked and how to train it to react differently.

In their book *The Whole-Brain Child*, Daniel J. Siegel, MD and Tina Payne Bryson, PhD teach about two different parts of the brain, "the upstairs brain and the downstairs brain." We can relate the upstairs brain with the prefrontal cortex, and we can relate the downstairs brain to the limbic system. This is a useful analogy when explaining how the brain works to children. "The jobs belonging to the downstairs brain are more primitive and often involve basic needs and instincts. The upstairs brain, on the other hand, is more sophisticated and responsible for many of the characteristics and behaviors we hope to see in our kids."

Siegel and Payne include this chart in *The Whole-Brain Child Workbook*, and it is helpful to illustrate how important it is to integrate both parts of the brain.

Downstairs Brain	Upstairs Brain
Fight/flight/ freeze response	Sound decision-making and planning
Autonomic function (breathing, blinking, instincts...)	Balancing emotions/ controlling body
Sensory memories	Self-understanding/ reflections
Strong emotions (fear, anger, excitement...)	Empathy
Acting before thinking	Morality

Siegel and Payne go on to point out at what age we can expect the upstairs part of our brain to be fully developed:

We have to remember that this upstairs brain doesn't complete its development until the mid-twenties, which means that it's vulnerable to not working well sometimes. With this in mind, kids and teens can't be expected to exhibit the sort of control over their bodies, emotions, and actions that adults can. Frankly, even with a fully developed upstairs brain, many adults don't have sufficient practice using it and still have difficulty accessing the skills associated with it!

Ditch the Double Standard

Throughout the years, teachers have pointed out that sometimes we have higher expectations for student behavior than we do for adult behavior. We teach children to say only nice things about each other and we teach them emotional regulation strategies to manage strong emotional reactions. All the while, we are gossiping about each other and flying off the handle when we are upset. Understanding how late the upstairs brain, or prefrontal cortex, develops makes this an even more unfair double standard. We are all human, we will make mistakes, we will act on our emotions, we will do hurtful things to each other. Then we will apologize, forgive ourselves, and strive to be better every day. We deserve grace, and our students do even more so.

We deserve grace, and our students do even more so.

The first step to lessening the intense reactions with Sam was to help him understand his own brain. From there, we practiced reflection and brainstormed strategies that could help him better control his response. Calming strategies like mindful breathing helped, as did physical strategies like taking a walk or replacement behavior strategy like practicing taking a deep breath and saying, "Okay" in response to directions. The practice started simply with Sam setting a goal to say, "Okay" one time per day because our goal is to help students experience small successes and build from there. Starting small and setting up students (and adults) for success allow for slow, steady, and consistent growth.

Trauma Comes in All Shapes and Sizes

Trauma can look different than we think or expect it to, and it is not limited to students or employees who show up with dirty hair and dirty clothes. Trauma can occur in the most unthinkable home environments and in homes that look perfectly polished.

The strategies we will discuss using the HANDLE acronym apply to all people, but they are even more important to use when we are supporting people who have experienced trauma. We know we will never know the background of all the people we encounter on a daily basis—whether they are people we meet face to face, the voice at the other end of the customer service phone line, our colleagues, friends, or the acquaintances with whom we interact on social media. Everyone has a story. Everyone has their own set of challenges, which is why we need to learn to HANDLE each other with care.

Serendipitous Lessons

- Trauma is not an event; it is the perception of an event.
- Traumatic events do not have to be traumatizing if a caring adult helps buffer the event.
- Trauma affects the brain in lasting and significant ways, and understanding this is the first step in lessening its impact.
- Not only do we have no right to hurt another person, we have a responsibility to help one another.
- The supports and strategies that help people who have been affected by trauma can actually help everyone.
- Even the telemarketer who calls during dinner is a person who deserves to be HANDLE'd with care. Every single person we interact with deserves it.

#SerendipityEDU

What new understanding did you develop about trauma, or what previous understanding was strengthened? How will this impact your daily interactions?

Share your story at #SerendipityEDU

Chapter 5

Hope Is Everything

*There was never a night or a problem
that could defeat sunrise or hope.*

—Bernard Williams

"**M**om, I don't want to go."

Annabelle rushes around the house, thinking to herself, *Ugh, are we really going to do this again? Sarah knows she has to go to her dad's house every other weekend. It has been this way for the past five years. But nearly every weekend, Sarah complains about having to go. I love her to pieces, but I could actually use the break this weekend. I am so drained, and I have zero patience left.*

Sarah walks up to Annabelle. She gets really close, and the mother and daughter meet eye to eye because Sarah is only a half-inch shy of being the same height as her mom. She says, "Mother, did you hear me? I don't want to go!"

Annabelle sighs loudly and replies, "Seriously, Sarah? Do we have to do this again? You *always* complain. If it isn't about having to spend the weekend at your dad's, then it is about what is for dinner. Or about school. Or whatever. I am sick of it."

Sarah looks at her mom with hurt and anger in her eyes. She bursts into tears and runs down the hall to her room and slams her door.

"You are right, Mom. I am a horrible person. Thank you for confirming that!" Sarah yells through her closed bedroom door.

Oh no, Annabelle thinks. *What have I done?*

• • •

Ouch. That story hurt a bit to write because I have made the same kind of mistake. I have completely missed the mark with what my child needs from me and instead reacted emotionally. Sarah was looking for hope from her mom. Annabelle not only didn't give her the hope about the weekend she was looking for, she helped Sarah feel worse about herself. Now Sarah is still dreading the weekend with her dad and thinks that she is a horrible person who is always complaining.

There are two things that bury hope alive, and Annabelle used both of them: emotion-filled words and absolutes. Emotion-filled words and phrases like "seriously?" and "sick of it" are so painful to hear. Our old childhood chant is wrong—words do hurt us.

Absolutes are words like "always" and "never," which propel problems from a level ten to a level one hundred in an instant because they make any issue seem much larger than it actually is. It feels significantly more difficult to try to solve a problem that *always* happens than to try to fix a one-time problem. Hope is alive and well with a small problem. It is crushed and buried and really hard to dig back up with huge problems.

Sarah's problem started off as just one problem. She didn't want to go to her dad's for the weekend. After the argument with her mom, she suddenly had an overwhelming number of issues crushing down on her: she still doesn't want to go to her dad's, she complains all the time, her mom is sick of her, and she must hate everything. She cannot possibly solve all of those problems, so hope is lost. Out the window.

Words have so much more power than we think. If you've been in a similar situation with your teen, as I have, you know that it's unlikely Sarah complains about *everything* or that her mom is sick of her (the complaining, sure, but not of her daughter whom she deeply loves). But those emotion-filled words and absolutes painted a hurtful picture and left Sarah (whose rational brain is still developing, remember) feeling hopeless.

Words have so much more power than we think.

Since this is a book and not real life, Annabelle gets a do-over. As you read this scenario, pay careful attention to how different it feels.

• • •

"Mom, I don't want to go."

Annabelle rushes around the house, thinking to herself, *Ugh, are we really going to do this again? Sarah knows that she has to go to her dad's house every other weekend. It has been this way for the past five years. But nearly every weekend, Sarah complains about having to go. I love her to pieces, but I could actually use the break this weekend. I am so drained, and I have zero patience left.*

Sarah walks up to Annabelle. She gets really close, and mother and daughter meet eye to eye because Sarah is only a half-inch shy of being the same height as her mom. She says, "Mother, did you hear me? I don't want to go!"

Instead of saying what she is thinking, Annabelle takes a deep breath, smiles slowly, and gently reminds her daughter, "I know, honey. But you have to go. Your dad loves you so much and is really looking forward to your weekend together. I am sure he has fun things planned."

Sarah looks at her mom with skepticism in her eyes. She shakes her head as she walks down the hall to her room.

"You are way too optimistic, Mom! It is going to be so boring," Sarah yells through her open bedroom door.

Someday, Annabelle thinks, *someday she will understand that looking on the bright side makes life so much easier.*

•   •   •

Goodness gracious, if we can keep a problem small, then let's keep it small! Hope is everything; it really is. When we have even an ember of hope in our hearts, we feel like we can conquer the world. When a huge boulder of a problem rolls over that hope and extinguishes it, we feel weak and conquered. In the do-over, Sarah walked into her room with more hope than she had before, even if she would never admit that to her mom. An interesting side effect is that Annabelle also had more hope. They kept the problem small and solvable. Sarah still wasn't looking forward to going to her dad's house, but Annabelle's words reminded her daughter that her dad loved her. In addition, Annabelle modeled the type of thinking that will help Sarah become an effective and fulfilled adult.

Not only is it extremely helpful to keep problems as small as possible, it is beneficial to break down big problems into small, easily solvable chunks. For example, I struggle with my weight. And when I say struggle, I mean *struggle*. It is a lifelong fight that started in elementary school, and I decided that I will never stop fighting. So I will struggle on. When I set a long-term goal for my weight, it seems insurmountable. It is hard to have hope when my goal is so big. But if I break down my goal into small daily or weekly milestones, I have hope because reaching them seems possible. Setting small, achievable goals is the only way I have been able to have some success.

So many things in life are out of our control, and there are so many things that we can never give to another person. As much as we may want to, we cannot, for example, give someone self-confidence. We cannot give a student's family stability. But there is something that we can always offer to the people in our lives: *hope*. Small gestures—a reminder of better times, a reassuring hand placed on the shoulder, or even a simple smile—can reignite the flame of hope in an instant.

There is something that we can always offer to the people in our lives: *hope*.

Serendipitous Lessons

- Hope is everything when it comes to solving problems.
- Avoiding emotion-filled words can help us keep hope alive.
- Absolutes like "always" and "never" often extinguish hope.
- Keep problems as small as possible, and break big problems down into small chunks.
- In real life, we don't get do-overs, so let's choose our words very carefully.
- Hope is something we *can* freely give to others.

#SerendipityEDU

Which strategies do you use when you need to reignite your ember of hope? How do you help the people around you feel hopeful? Share your story with us. We are better together.

Share your story at #SerendipityEDU

Chapter 6
Assure Safety:
Let Me Be Your Shield

Your spirit is the true shield.

—Morihei Ueshiba

Let Me Be Your Shield

Our hearts break when we hear about
the challenges you face at home.

We see the sadness in your eyes and
the slump of your shoulders.

It feels like there is nothing we
can do to help you.

We can't stop your mom and dad
from fighting each night.

But we can hug you and say, "I am so happy
you are here," when you arrive every morning.

We cannot make sure that you eat
warm and nutritious dinners.

We can make sure you are never
hungry when you are at school.

Your mom doesn't pamper you and gently
comb your hair each morning.

But a hairbrush and pretty bows can
be waiting for you at school.

We can't keep your house neat and clean or
keep your laundry freshly washed and folded.

However, clean clothes can be ready for you at
school so you feel like the beautiful girl you are.

We cannot make you feel safe
at night at your house.

We can make sure that you are continually
reminded how strong you are.

Sometimes you feel like you are what they
call you, that you are dumb and worthless.

But you can blossom at school and
discover who you really are.

Your family may feel stuck and hopeless.

We can help you understand that there is
a whole world waiting for you with
unlimited possibilities for your future.

We cannot fix things that are
beyond our control.

But we can take advantage of all
of our minutes together.

To be a shield against the scary things you see.

To help you believe in yourself and
have hope for your future.

To help you feel strong and to know your value.

Now that we think about it,

There is so much we can do for you.

We can be your shield.

Assure Safety

The "A" in HANDLE stands for *Assure safety*. The ultimate goal is to have our presence communicate safety to others—to say, "You are safe with me. I will not hurt you. I will shield you from pain when I can."

As a school principal, I want my presence to communicate safety to my students and staff, to our school's families, and to the greater community. As a mom, I want my presence to communicate safety to my sons. The same applies to all relationships in my life—as a wife, as a daughter, as a sister, as a friend. I want others to feel safer, not just physically but emotionally as well, because I am around.

> I want others to feel safer, not just physically but emotionally as well, because I am around.

In the five basic needs that Dr. Glasser identified, survival is directly tied to safety. At a primary level, people need to feel all the elements of physical safety. We need enough food, we need shelter, we need water, and we need basic hygiene. If those needs are not met, nothing else matters because we are too busy trying to keep ourselves alive. That is why, at school, we work to ensue those basic survival needs are met by supplying food and water. But remember, these needs are not exclusive to students in school. That grumpy woman behind you in line at the gas station? It could be that she is grumpy because she is hungry, dehydrated, or sleeping in her car.

In addition to the need for physical safety, all humans have a need to feel emotionally safe. For people who have been through trauma, that kind of safety can seem difficult to find. Have you ever been around someone who is hyper aware of his or her environment? Every unexpected noise makes that person look for threats. Individuals who have experienced trauma, especially repeated trauma, often are so focused on their safety that the limbic system of their brain reacts quickly and intensely to help them stay safe. The supports these individuals need differ because of their unique experiences, but there are some universal supports that may help them and everyone we encounter.

Let's go back to Allie's story to consider supports that might help her.

• • •

After Allie walked out of the party, she turned down the hallway leading to her office. She sighed with relief just as she was about to enter her cocoon of safety when she heard someone say, "Not feeling like partying today, eh?"

Allie turned around to see Seth, the new guy at the office. He seemed so outgoing and friendly, so she was surprised that he wasn't enjoying the social time with their colleagues.

"I went to the party for a few minutes, but I have a ton of work to get done tonight. I am going to try to cross a couple more things off my to-do list before I head home. You should head there. They always have delicious cake, and it is a good opportunity for you to get to know people better." Allie smiled as she encouraged him.

Seth could see Allie's struggle in their workplace. He also knew that there was more to Allie's story. He saw her hightail it out of the party looking distraught, and he hoped to connect with her and maybe even make her feel better. He wasn't sure how, so he decided to ask for her help.

"I will head down there in a few minutes. Can I ask you a couple questions about something I am working on first?" Seth asked.

"Sure, no problem." Allie was glad to help. *Maybe Seth is a good guy*, she thought. *It would be so nice to have a friend at work.* Allie longed to connect with someone who did not have a hidden agenda, someone she could feel safe around. Allie was typically leery of guys because she had been burned many times by men's hidden agendas. She didn't get that vibe from Seth, though. It was refreshing.

Allie reminded Seth of a friend of his from college who had a similar guard up when he had met her. He knew the effort it was going to take to help Allie see that she didn't have to have her shield up with everyone. He also knew from experience that the friendship and collegiality they could forge after she took down her guard would be worth the work and could even give Allie hope in people again. Even without knowing her whole story, Seth understood that Allie would never feel safe with anyone until she learned to be confident in herself. He hoped he could help her see that the behavior of their cliquish colleagues had nothing to do with Allie and everything to do with them.

Over time, Seth helped lighten Allie's load. Their interaction gave her hope that she might be able to establish a safe and trusting relationship at work. His easygoing manner and the fact that he sought out Allie for guidance helped her see the workplace a little differently. Before too long, she began to see Seth as a trusted colleague.

• • •

Relationships are two-way streets, and in order for both Seth and Allie to feel safe with each other, Allie will have to reciprocate the intentional relationship-building with Seth.

Who did you think of as you read about the interaction between Seth and Allie? Who in your life has their guard up? Who in your life might need the same supports that Allie needs? Which things do we need to consider as we work to assure safety with the people who need it the most?

- Notice how they are feeling by making observations and then asking about it. Sometimes we are worried we will offend people when we say things like, "I notice you seem upset. Is there anything I can do to help?" But when we avoid emotion-filled words, absolutes, and judgment, we often avoid offending others.
- Build the relationship carefully and slowly, getting to know each other before making assumptions about what they need and how we can help them feel safe.
- Be consistent and predictable so they know what to expect from us.
- Empower them by seeking their guidance and asking for help. When people have their guards up, they often cannot contribute to relationships in the way they want to, so allowing them to contribute in other ways helps them feel like equal partners in the relationship.
- Be careful not to take personal offense when they put up walls or take steps back in the relationship. Even when they pull back, our best move is to continue being our caring and consistent selves.

That last bullet point may be the most important one. People who have faced trauma and difficulties in their lives will put up defenses when they get scared. They may pull back from the relationship or get defensive at seemingly innocuous comments. We might not know the triggers for the people around us, but we do know that defensiveness is a potential indicator of lack of emotional safety and a "fight or flight" reaction.

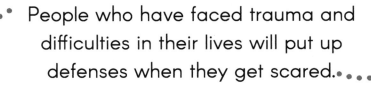

People who have faced trauma and difficulties in their lives will put up defenses when they get scared.

My encouragement to you is to not take defensive behavior personally. In truth, how others behave tells us very little about how they feel about us but tells us so much about how they feel about themselves. Choose not to respond to defensiveness with defensiveness. Instead, respond with compassion. Be true to yourself and believe that the best you can do is good enough.

Serendipitous Lessons

- Assuring the physical and emotional safety of others is an important part of being compassionate.
- Our words, our body language, and our behavior can communicate safety to others.
- Asking others for help can help communicate safety in a relationship.
- Defensiveness is a potential indicator of lack of emotional safety.
- Avoid responding to defensiveness with defensiveness by understanding that others' behavior is typically not about you.

#SerendipityEDU

How do others know that they are safe in your presence? Which actions communicate physical safety, and which actions communicate emotional safety? Which goals did you set for yourself after reading this chapter?

Share your story at #SerendipityEDU

Chapter 7
No Shoulda' Needed

*If you judge people, you have
no time to love them.*

—Mother Teresa

D o you love it when people tell you what you "should have done"?
No, we typically hate it! When I was first learning Choice
Theory, I had a trainer named Jeanette McDaniel. She is this incredibly sweet powerhouse of a woman with the best Southern drawl. We
giggled like crazy when she told us not to "shoulda' all over everyone."
It is funny to think of it that way, but it is so true. When we shoulda' all
over others, we are implying something negative. Saying, "You should
have done this," is saying, "You were wrong," and "I know better than
you." Even worse, we often shoulda' on people before we ask questions
or learn enough about the situation to make an informed judgement.

The "N" in the HANDLE acronym stands for *No shoulda' needed*,
and to be safe rather than sorry on this one, we might just want to
simply wipe the word "should" from our vocabulary entirely. I have
been working to replace "should" with words like "could" or "might,"
and it is not easy, but it is possible. Replacing a judgment-filled word
like "should" with words that are more open can lead to great discus-
sions rather than defensiveness. Choosing our words carefully is an

important part of being compassionate and people centered. There are many words that we use pretty freely that have big emotional implications, and, believe it or not, "should" is one of those words. People don't need our judgment; they need our love and support. That does not mean that we never tell others what we think or how we feel. Instead, it means that we only tell others what we think and how we feel if it will help them and if they want that kind of input.

> People don't need our judgement; they need our love and support.

I Shoulda' All Over Myself

The one person we all shoulda' on the most is ourselves. From the time we wake up saying, "Oh, I should have gotten more sleep last night," to the time we go to bed thinking, "I should have done this or that today," we tend to constantly shoulda' all over ourselves. It is just as important to wipe the word "should" out of our self-talk because it prohibits growth and keeps us stuck in some harmful patterns of behavior.

The same guidelines that apply to our conversations with others apply to our conversations with ourselves. Surfer Laird Hamilton is credited with saying, "Make sure your worst enemy doesn't live between your own two ears." How is it that we are okay with saying things to ourselves that we would never even imagine saying to someone else? The words we tell ourselves have even more power than the words we tell others. The battle is hard, but it is so worth the fight—let's be our own hero rather than our own enemy. Let's be our own biggest fans because if we don't believe in ourselves, how can we expect others to believe in us? Oh my dear friends, believe me when I tell you that I write this for myself just as much as I write it for you.

The words we tell ourselves have even more power than the words we tell others.

One of my morning rituals is listening to inspiring videos, podcasts, or books that will help me prioritize *who* I need to be to make the most out of the day over *what* I need to accomplish. Educational leader Lisa Dabbs introduced me to a motivational YouTube video that includes a moving speech about the power of what follows "I am..." by pastor Joel Osteen.

> Whatever follows your "I am" will always come looking for you—you're handing it an invitation, opening the door, and giving it permission to be in your life. The good news is you get to choose what follows "I am." Go through the day saying, "I am blessed," and blessings will come looking for you. Declare, "I am talented," and talent will come looking for you. You may not feel up to par, but when you say it, you're inviting that into your life.

What are you inviting into your life? What follows your "I am"?

I am so grateful? I am so strong? I am more than enough? I am better every day?

Let's all take a moment to think about the amazing people we are, and the even more amazing people we are working to become.

Replace Judgment with Hopeful Curiosity

Even when someone asks us, "What should I do?" let's try not to respond with, "You should...". We could respond with some different options as we see them, or suggest something that they *could* do. Not only does that feel better, it helps keep the ownership of the decision on the person who needs to make the decision. It communicates support without shifting the responsibility.

Here are some shoulda' replacements you could consider using (notice what I did there?):

"I wonder..."

"What if..."

"Could you..."

"What have you tried so far?"

"Can you think of anything that worked in the past?"

"Maybe..."

"What do you think about..."

"Might you..."

"What have you considered?"

Let's change our judgmental thoughts into hopeful curiosity. Let's start our thoughts with *I wonder...* and end them with *I bet it will work out...*

Let's change our judgmental
thoughts into hopeful curiosity.

Serendipitous Lessons

- No shoulda' on anyone is a great rule of thumb. No one likes to be told what they "should do"—it is crippling and can inadvertently shift responsibility for behavior. *Should* can be changed to *could* in almost every situation.
- Let's swap out judgmental thoughts with hopeful curiosity.
- While we are at it, let's do these things for ourselves too. No shoulda' self-talk or unfair judgements of ourselves.
- If we don't believe in ourselves, how can we expect others to believe in us?
- I really, *really* wish I had a Southern drawl, y'all. I try, but I sound ridiculous. Want proof? Check out my YouTube channel!

#SerendipityEDU

I would love to hear your ideas to avoid "shoulda" and instead invite hopeful curiosity into your life. Which connections did you make to this chapter? What follows your "I am..."?

Share your story at #SerendipityEDU

Chapter 8
Take Control, Be Different

If you want something you have never had, you must be willing to do something you have never done.

—Thomas Jefferson

Years ago on the ride home from school, one of my boys, who was just five at the time, told me all about the difficulties he'd had on the playground that day. After he lamented about how horribly he had been treated by some of his friends, I said, "Buddy, this is going to be a little hard to hear, and it is something that many adults don't even know. But, I know a secret to living a happy life. Do you think you are old enough to hear this secret?"

He nodded and he looked at me with expectation. He wanted in on the secret. Little did he know that this secret, although accurate and important, is something that people choose to deny, fight against, and even start wars over.

"Okay, I think you are ready. Here it is: The only person you can control is *you*. This means that even if those boys are being very mean and what they are doing is wrong, you cannot change them. You can only change you. So, if you'd like the situation to get better, what do you think you could do to help it?"

He went on to share some ideas of things that he could do to change the boys. Maybe he could be very nice to them, and then they would change. Maybe he could tell a teacher. Maybe he could use kind words to ask the boys to stop what they were doing.

"You could do those things, and maybe they would work," I agreed. "The important part of this message is that you cannot change others. Only they can decide to do that. You can only change yourself."

This truth can be difficult to accept—even for adults. It's frustrating to know that even when you are doing absolutely the right thing, someone else may choose to do the absolutely wrong thing, and if you want the situation to change, *you* have to be the one to change. That doesn't seem fair at all, but it is the way life works. If you wait for the world to change for you, you may wait forever. Some people never understand this and spend their entire lives pretty unhappy as they wait for others to change.

If you wait for the world to change for you, you may wait forever.

My son and I talked a bit more and then I asked him, "If you'd like things to get better right away, how could you make a change that you have control over? What could you do?"

He decided he could walk away, find other people to play with, and try not to get upset when his friends were not being kind. He knew that he could turn to an adult at school if things got bad, but the challenges he was facing were ones he would face for the rest of his life. I wanted him to get some practice resolving issues on his own, beginning at this young age.

I will never claim to be a parenting guru. I have had my share of parenting ups and downs, and I will continue to have them. This is one lesson, however, that I am glad I took the opportunity to teach my boys. We all have more control over our lives than we believe. And from a young age, all people deserve the opportunity to learn that there is so much within their control: their actions and their thinking, and through those two things they can control much of how they feel. Waiting for others to change is a losing battle. Change will not come if we wait for some other person or some other time.

> *We are the ones we've been waiting for.*
>
> *—June Jordan*

You might be thinking, *But, wait! We expect children to learn this concept that so many adults haven't mastered?* Seems crazy, doesn't it? Then, maybe it is time for us adults to set the example by internalizing this lesson as well. If we want things to be different, we have to be different.

The "D" in the HANDLE acronym stands for *Do things differently.* If we want different relationships, we have to be different. If we want to achieve different goals, we have to be different. If we want to feel differently about our lives or about ourselves, we have to think and behave differently. If we want to support those we love in a different way, we have to treat them differently. It sounds so easy! Change only happens when we become aware of changes we can make and then intentionally choose to become difference makers.

Let's look at how this concept of being different applies to Allie's story. Allie's experiences left her feeling unsure of the world around her. Dr. Adolph Brown, thought leader, author, and humorist, talks about the emotional struggles we carry around like backpacks. Allie carried her heavy backpack everywhere she went. But the reality is that for life to be different—lighter—she has to be different. She cannot continue to look at the world around her through the same lens and expect different results.

· · ·

The day that Allie connected with Seth after the birthday party disaster, she flopped onto her couch as soon as she got home. Reflecting on the emotional roller coaster she had gone through, she considered how scared and intimidated she had felt at the birthday party—so much so that she wanted out of there as fast as she could. Then she had felt a sense of warmth and connection with Seth. She had found herself warming up to him so quickly, it surprised her. She was used to being closed off and cautious with people.

But, Allie thought that day, *where is that getting me? I am constantly watching my back. I have my guard up at every turn. Yes, very bad things have happened in my life. But I can't change my past. It will always be there, and it will always be a part of me. I can, however, change my future. I don't want to live like this anymore. I have tried to change my environment. I have tried to change the people around me. But, ultimately, it is not them who needs to change. It is me. I am the only person I can control, and I am the only person who can change the way I am living my life.*

Those few moments of reflection had caught her off guard. Where had that sudden introspectiveness come from? Maybe it was the hope that the interaction with Seth provided? Maybe she was growing up? Or, maybe she was finally sick of living like a caged lion. For the first time, she knew she was ready to break free from the protective shelter she had built for herself. It had been useful at the time, but rather than providing protection, it was providing a barrier between Allie and others. Allie knew that she would never realize all that she could become and do while she had so many walls up.

Okay, what is the first step? she asked herself. *Tomorrow, I am going to look at the people at work differently. I am going to assume that they want good things for themselves and for others. Even for me. They just don't know how to make it all happen. They are in the same struggle as I am. And who knows, maybe they have gone through traumatic experiences themselves. Who am I to judge them? Starting tomorrow, I will open my heart to them. Just a little. And I will open my heart a little more every day. It will hurt, and it will be hard, but it will be worth it.*

• • •

Recognizing the roadblocks we have set up for ourselves is the first step in looking at the world through a different lens. A roadblock I have identified for myself is that I allow the emotions of others to trip me up. I want everyone around me to be happy and to be loving life, and when they aren't, I have a tendency to take on their emotions. That is why I invented the "Emotions Deflector" to help with this problem. When I wear my Emotions Deflector, the emotions of others bounce right off me and back to them. I can empathize and understand what they are feeling and why, and I can ask them how I can help, but I do not take on their emotions. The crazy thing is

Recognizing the roadblocks we have set up for ourselves is the first step in looking at the world through a different lens.

that it helps both the other person and me when I don't take on their emotions. It helps me think rationally, and it helps me be more empathetic because I am focused on the other person rather than how I am feeling. Of course, both of these things are helpful to the other person, too.

> *When little people are overwhelmed*
> *by big emotions, it's our job to share*
> *our calm, not join their chaos.*
>
> *—L. R. Knost*

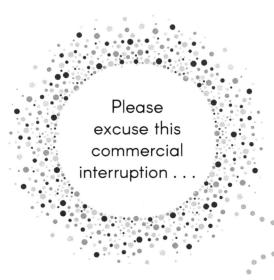

Please
excuse this
commercial
interruption . . .

Buy the  Today!
NEW and Improved

One moment you are approaching your day with a cheery disposition... and BOOM! You run into someone who woke up on the wrong side of the bed. You walk away from their grumbling with a lump in your stomach and realize you've lost the bounce in your step.

But don't worry!

The new and improved Emotions Deflector is now available! Like the popular first version, our new Emotions Deflector will allow you to walk away from Mr. Grumpypants with the same cheery disposition you had before your encounter with him.

This special, improved version allows you to deflect negative emotions without interfering with empathy. You can still feel *with* people, but you don't take on their emotions when you are wearing your Emotions Deflector.

For a low, low cost of four payments of $9.99 plus shipping and handling, you can purchase the
Amazing Emotions Deflector *today!*

 No longer will you succumb to the emotions of Mr. Grumpypants.

 No longer will Mrs. ComplainsAllTheTime ruin your happy mood!

If you act now, a special bonus will be thrown in!

Your smile and cheery disposition will positively affect Mr. Grumpypants, and you might even turn his day around! This two-for-one special won't last! Act today to get your very own Emotions Deflector!

Understanding and Using Recent Bias to Be Different

My brother, bless his heart, allows me to wax philosophic with him. In a phone conversation not long ago, we got on the subject of recent bias—the idea that things that have happened most recently carry more significance than things that happened over and over again for months or even years.

This phenomenon of recent bias shows up frequently in education. A teacher will tell me, "Oh my goodness, Allyson, Peter is really struggling to get along with his classmates. He has been struggling all year. I don't know what to do with him." But that same teacher told me just two weeks before that Peter was doing really well and that he had made so much progress during the past few months.

I can imagine this same thing happening at the chemical plant where my brother, Todd, is the manager.

"I don't know what to do, Todd. Daniel is falling apart. He cannot run his machine properly. He has had challenges all year. I am out of ideas to help him."

In this fictional example, my brother thinks back to the month before, when this same supervisor came to him raving about what a good job Daniel was doing. What had changed? Well, Daniel made two mistakes in a row, and in this supervisor's mind, he was falling apart. The two mistakes, although relatively minor, practically erased the months of outstanding work that happened before the mistakes.

What causes this misperception or distortion of reality?

Recent bias. Recent events tend to carry the most weight in our minds. Something could have happened once or twice recently, and in our minds that thing becomes the norm—something that *always* happens. It is one of the tricks our minds play on us, and it is an important one to recognize. Remember when we talked about absolutes in Chapter 5? When a problem suddenly becomes "always" or "never," it suddenly feels too big to solve. If we can help ourselves keep problems in perspective and keep them as small as possible, they can be solved much easier.

Recent events tend to carry the most weight in our minds.

In doing some research, I discovered the technical term for recent bias is "the bias of availability heuristic," and it means that we have a bias to use the information most readily available to us to make decisions or judgements. The most readily available information is often the most recent information, which explains why we often place the most weight on recent incidents when making a judgement.

When we think about being different, it is essential that we consider whether the bias of availability heuristic is preventing us from making accurate judgements. In order to stay in our "upstairs brain" or our prefrontal cortex and stall an automatic fight, flight, or freeze response from the limbic system, we need to take into account all the information available to us—not just the most recent data. By understanding the bias of availability heuristic, we are able to...

- Look for overarching patterns of behavior rather than just focusing on recent events.
- Look for times when things were better, and we can then analyze the circumstances that helped them be better. Often if we try to replicate those circumstances, things do get better again.
- Understand the size of the problem. Is this in fact a long-standing problem? Or did it happen a long time ago

and now it is recurring? Or is it a little blip that can easily be solved?

- Look at how we are feeling in a different way, and we know that to get different results, we have to do things differently.

Let's look at the availability heuristic bias with a different lens. Could this bias work *for* us? This bias is evidence that what has happened most recently bears significantly more weight on our perceptions. So if we are feeling badly about ourselves for some reason, could we feel better almost immediately after taking some quick action? When I think of this, my mind goes back to that area where I constantly struggle—eating healthily. I could go for months eating mostly candy and fried foods. I could then spend two days eating healthily, and all of a sudden, I change my perception of how I take care of myself—I become a healthy eating expert qualified to give advice. Recent bias helps us understand that changing what we are doing changes how we think, and our feelings follow along.

I am certainly not a cognitive psychologist, and I really don't even understand what "heuristic" means. To ease my feeble brain, let's agree to call it the "recent bias" instead of the "availability heuristic" bias. One thing I know for sure—I am better equipped to make different choices because I understand this bias.

Want to learn more about recent bias?
Check out this article by Kendra Cherry at:
verywellmind.com/availability-heuristic-2794824.

Serendipitous Lessons

- If we want different results, we have to be different.
- Understanding that everyone has their own story helps us look at others through a different lens.
- Assuming that others want good things for themselves—and for everyone around them—helps everyone.
- Wear your Emotions Deflector to not only help yourself but to also better help others.
- Understanding our bias toward recent events helps us problem-solve with more accurate data.
- My brother is a saint for indulging my philosophical rants. Love him!

#SerendipityEDU

As you read this chapter, which area of your life are you thinking about? What would you like to be different in your personal or professional life? Which changes might you make to start that process?

Share your story at #SerendipityEDU

Chapter 9
Listen to Understand

Listening, not imitation, may be
the sincerest form of flattery.

—Dr. Joyce Brothers

We could blame the lack of listening on all the noise in our world today. Consider the sources of noises blaring at any given time in any typical American household. Television, video games, music, and streaming YouTube videos flood our environments with noise. We listen to lots of stuff. Lack of listening is not the problem. Lack of empathetic listening to understand each other is. And I am as guilty of it as you are.

We moved during the summer before my oldest son entered eighth grade. We were living in Traverse City, Michigan, and moved two and a half hours away so I could be a principal in Zeeland, Michigan, near Grand Rapids. My husband and I had grown up in Grand Rapids, and we were moving back near family and friends. Our oldest son was involved in the steps that led up to the decision to move. We talked through the possibility of the move as I applied for jobs and what worried him and what excited him about it. He was excited to live near family and about the things the city had to offer.

He was not opposed to the idea of a new school but a bit nervous about the fresh start. Although he was sad and a little scared, he rolled with the punches pretty well during the process.

As a parent, I believe that challenges are good for our children. I want to allow my boys to go through difficult things while they are still in my household, where we can work through the challenges together. With that idea in mind, I approached our family's move with the attitude that "what doesn't kill us makes us stronger." What I needed to take into consideration, though, was that we can never neglect to listen to the struggles of the people around us. Their struggles are real, and they need to be acknowledged. We can't wish them away. Once we notice the struggles and validate them, we can work through them. I learned this the hard way, which, unfortunately, is how I learn most things.

> Once we notice the struggles
> and validate them, we can
> work through them.

Three years after our move, we were having dinner one evening and our eleventh-grade son made an announcement. He said, "For the first time since we moved, I feel good about myself." My jaw dropped. Silently I yelled, *Ummm . . . what?!? You haven't felt good about yourself for three years?* My heart breaks just thinking about that. In my effort to rush around trying to make everything okay with everyone, I neglected to notice just how badly my son was feeling. I didn't see how significantly the move affected him. I didn't listen to understand; I didn't dig deep enough.

We have 20/20 vision when we look back on life, so *now* I can easily see why he was so significantly impacted by the move. His world was turned upside down in so many ways. He went to the same school from preschool through seventh grade. I was a principal at his school that entire time. It was a small school where he knew everyone, and many people there were like family. I just plucked him out of that nurturing environment and had him start fresh in a bigger school where he knew no one. And I wasn't at the school with him. Not only was he not surrounded by people who were like family, he was the outsider now. No wonder he would rarely leave the house when he wasn't in school. He needed the safe cocoon of our family and our home.

Our younger son was able to go to the school where I was the principal, and he transitioned in second grade, which was so much easier than transitioning in middle school. He not only survived the move well, he thrived. When I look back at those years when our older son was struggling, I wonder how I could have better listened to understand. How can I turn my terrible parenting into three easy steps to listen better? I can't. But I can and I will learn from it. The L in our HANDLE acronym stands for *Listen to understand*, and it takes time, silence, questions, perspective, and empathy to be a good listener.

Listening to understand takes time—slow, deliberate, dedicated time to listen to really hear and empathize. Put away all the distractions. Flip your phone over and make sure it is on do not disturb, close your laptop, shut the door, or go for a walk together to chat. Do what you need to do to make sure your focus can be on the person right in front of you. Listen with your eyes, your ears, your brain, and your heart.

Listening to understand takes silence. If you are really listening to someone, you will need to pause when he or she is done speaking in order to consider how to best respond. You cannot *really* listen if you are formulating your response while the other person is talking.

To make the silence more comfortable and less awkward for every-one, set the expectation for it by saying something like, "I am going to be listening to you carefully, so I will pause before I respond so I am not thinking of my response while you are talking."

Listening to understand takes questions. You can build trust and demonstrate good listening by paraphrasing what the person has said. After confirming your understanding by paraphrasing, ask a question. Just one question, not a series of them. You don't need to state the same question three different ways. Just ask one thoughtful question to deepen your understanding. With our son, I could have said, "That is a long time to feel badly about yourself. What changed recently to help you feel better?"

Listening to understand is not about you. It is human nature to want to interject your own experiences or compare your life to the other person's life. Listening to understand is about the person in front of you. You can share stories that relate to the other person's story when it will specifically benefit that person, but sharing is not always caring when it comes to listening. Be careful not to inadvertently turn the spotlight on yourself and leave the other person thinking, *Okay . . . I thought we were talking about me? Now it is about you?*

Listening to understand is empathetic, not sympathetic. In *The Path to Serendipity*, I shared three "don'ts" for being empathetic.

1. ***Don't put yourself in others' shoes*** because you will end up with more than just stinky feet. You will end up with an inaccurate perception of the problem. It is not about how *you* would feel or handle the problem. It is about how they feel and how they might best handle the problem. I did not have the same experiences as my son, so I could not simply put myself in his shoes and expect to understand how he felt.

2. ***Don't kick people when they are down*** by making a judgement. Accurate or not, they just don't need your judgement. They need your love and support. Don't shoulda' all over them.

3. ***Don't assume you know how to help.*** Instead, ask four very important words, "How can I help?"

Here is a crazy, mind-blowing thing—are you ready for it? People need us to be good listeners when things are going amazingly well just as much as when they are going amazingly bad. I didn't really understand this one until I experienced it myself.

So I think you guys are picking up on the fact that I wrote a book called *The Path to Serendipity*. It was a dream-I-never-even-dared-to-dream come true. Like, I couldn't even call myself an author until I was holding it in my hands because I just couldn't believe that it was actually happening. I was so excited, and I had tears in my eyes every time I thought about being an actual published author and being able to share the things I hold closest to my heart with the world. I still can't believe it.

I try not to be petty or selfish, so what I am about to share is not something I dwell on, but it is something I felt strongly in the moment, and I always want to learn from strong feelings. There were many times that I would tell people I love and care about that I was publishing a book and the response would be, "That's really cool," and then they would change the subject. This happened with colleagues, family members, friends, you name it. I was feeling that "*This is the most amazing thing that I never thought would ever, ever happen and I can't believe it is happening*" feeling, and I wanted the people I love to understand how I was feeling and to feel *with* me. Feeling with people, as Brené Brown has taught us, is what empathy is all about. I wanted my family, friends, and colleagues to empathize with me in that spectacular moment. But, in many cases, they didn't.

What stopped them from sharing in my excitement? It wasn't because they don't love me, because I know they do. It wasn't because they weren't happy for me, because they likely were. I think it is because we don't universally understand the importance of listening to understand when things are going great. I didn't even understand that until I experienced how lack of empathy during the good times feels. It is absolutely astonishing that the same don'ts for being empathetic apply just as much when things are going well as they apply when things are going badly. Take a few seconds to flip back to the page where those don'ts are listed and reread them with this new lens. Don't worry, I'll wait.

> We don't universally understand the importance of listening to understand when things are going great.

I told you! Eye-opening, isn't it? Now, think of someone in your life who is super passionate about something that you are totally uninterested in. My oldest son, for example, was super passionate about video games. His dad and I fought against video games for years as we have encouraged him to find balance, explore other interests, and put limits on his use. If that is all we did, we were not HANDLE-ing our son with care because we were not listening to understand. Video games were his biggest passion for a few years, and in order to continue to have a positive and effective relationship with him, it was important for us to listen to understand and to avoid those three don'ts.

Every person in your life is passionate about something, or may have an exciting thing happening in his/her life. Maybe they are moving to their dream house or learning a new skill. Or maybe they have accomplished a long-term goal or had a new baby or grandchild. Whatever it is, be sure to listen to understand through the good and the bad so you can empathize with their joy with as much care as you do their sorrow.

Where Does Social Media Fit in to "Listening to Understand"?

I was a social media avoider for years. I didn't even have a Facebook account until the spring of 2017. I was scared—scared of comparing myself to others and scared that I would feel like I wasn't good enough when I saw the amazing things other people were doing. I was also scared that I would fall into a trap, trying to make my life look perfect. I was scared, but I was wrong.

Social media has just as much power to do good in the world as it does to do bad. We can help others feel like they are not alone, we can share our stories in hopes that it will inspire and uplift, we can learn from what other people share, we can celebrate and support other people. We can do so much good with just a few clicks. We can do so much bad with just a few clicks, too—so pull your hands away from that keyboard when you are feeling upset and are about to post something.

As each new year approaches, I reflect on all I learned the past year, and I set a focus for the year ahead. For 2018, I decided that I would work on celebrating others' successes as if they were my own. I knew in my heart that there was enough success for everyone, but often I would still feel threatened by others' achievements. That simple goal opened my heart big time. Being mindful of not only recognizing others' successes but giving them a whooping "WOOHOO!" has made me a better person. It is so important, even on social media, to spend just as much time "listening" as we do posting our own good news.

Empathy applies to social media—how can we show others that we feel with them via social media? How can we HANDLE each other with care even when communicating digitally? Retweet that great blogpost, make that positive comment, give uplifting messages frequently, if for no other reason than because they are a boomerang. The more celebrating you do of others, the more you will have to celebrate yourself.

Serendipitous Lessons

- We are good listeners. Listening is not the problem; listening to understand each other is.
- Listening to understand takes time, silence, questions, perspective, and empathy.
- The people in our lives deserve us to be empathetic through amazing triumph, devastating losses, and everything in between.
- The three don'ts of empathy apply to the good news as much as the bad news.
- When we wish people would treat us a certain way, it is good practice to turn the magnifying glass back on ourselves. Are you treating people the way you want to be treated?
- I apologize to my sons for learning on the job as I parent them. Mommy loves you!
- Social media has the power to do great things for us and for the people we love. Don't be afraid to use it to celebrate others' achievements. You will get so much back in return!

#SerendipityEDU

What personal connection did you make to the idea of listening carefully? Which ideas did you develop as you thought about the need to be just as good of a listener during the good times as we are during the bad times?

Share your story at #SerendipityEDU

Chapter 10
Establish, Then Keep, Trust

*Trust is the glue of life. It's the most
essential ingredient in effective
communication. It's the foundational
principle that holds all relationships.*

—Stephen R. Covey

When we last heard from Allie, she was giving herself a pep
talk before bed, determined to open her heart to her coworkers. She identified that she was doing the very same thing that they
were doing: she was judging them without really getting to know
them. Let's go back to her story to see if she wakes up with the
same determination.

• • •

Allie woke up feeling the same butterflies of hope in her stomach
that soothed her to sleep the night before. She felt empowered by her
realization that there is so much more within her control than she
previously understood. She practiced her best welcoming smile in the
mirror as she got ready for work. She put on her brightest outfit, which
unfortunately was a white shirt with gray pants. She laughed at herself, thinking that she needed to go shopping for clothes in brighter

colors. Then, her nerves started getting the best of her. She started asking herself questions like, *What if I try and they laugh at me?*

Then the tiniest voice of confidence spoke up. *No, Allie, you are* not *going to do this to yourself. You know that if you change, the world around you changes. Heaven knows you cannot control those cliques at the office, but you can control yourself. How about this: how about you start small today?* Allie felt hope return at the thought of taking one small step today and another small step tomorrow. She knew that, eventually, those small steps would lead to the big changes she wanted to see.

Allie understood that the girls in her office didn't trust her. She wasn't sure exactly why that was the case, but she was willing to guess that it was because they didn't know her. They didn't know that she wanted for good things for them—for everyone around her. The question was, how could she begin to establish trusting relationships with them? *Maybe*, she thought, *I can reach out to just one of them, the person who seems most open.* Allie pictured a colleague named Tinisha, who smiled easily and seemed genuine. Tinisha was one of the quieter members of the clique and seemed like she might be an easy person to talk to.

Okay, how do I even start? Allie wondered. *I could ask her about the Higgins deal. I have some questions about the work I am doing. Maybe I could email her to see if she has ideas? No, it would be better to visit her and ask her in person. That's what I'll do. Right away this morning, before I chicken out.*

• • •

We don't have to know everything about someone in order to trust them, but we do need to know what they value. And we need to know that they value us. Allie's plan is a solid start. Asking someone for help communicates the fact that you value the other person. It may take time for that person to open up to you, so don't give up after just one try. Trust may come last in the HANDLE acronym, but it has to come first with relationships. It is challenging and time-consuming to establish trust, but it takes just one mistake to break it. It is worth the intentional effort required to establish trust, and the continual effort it takes to maintain it. Here are a few ways to help establish it with others:

- **Communicate that you value the person.** First take the time to find out what he/she values. Then, show the person that you value him/her by asking for help or complimenting an achievement. The more specific you are, the stronger the message. Saying, "Wow! You really wrote a terrific email to that customer. Do you mind if I have you look over an email I want to send today?" is way more powerful a compliment than, "You look really nice today."

- **Share what you value.** Once you find out what the other person values, from really important things like the character traits they most highly value in another person to their favorite types of food, you can make connections to the things that you value. To establish a trusting relationship, you have to know each other well enough to understand each other's values.

- **Be playful.** This may sound like strange advice on a list of how to establish trusting relationships, but laughing with someone is one of the best ways to build trust. When we are playful with others, we demonstrate that we are comfortable enough to let down our guards. When we laugh together, we are strengthening our relationships. We are also sharing more of ourselves through our sense of humor. Just image how quickly Allie and Tinisha will bond if they share laughter within one of their first few interactions.

- **Act with integrity.** When someone gossips about someone else to us, it's almost impossible not think, *Uh-oh, I can only imagine what this person is saying to others about me behind my back.* In the moment, it seems easy to bond over juicy gossip, but in reality it deteriorates positive relationships and destroys trust. When someone gossips to you, you can pull out your Naive Body Spray (see the ad for ordering instructions) and assume they want good things for others and don't understand the negative impact of gossip. You could say, "So-and-so's feelings might be hurt if she heard you say that. I know you wouldn't want to hurt her feelings."

Another part of acting with integrity is being consistent. If Allie is friendly with Tinisha one day and standoffish the next, Tinisha will be leery of Allie, and any trust will quickly erode.

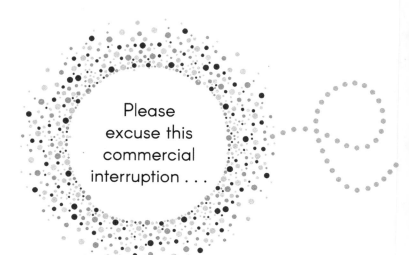

Please excuse this commercial interruption . . .

Naive Body Spray

Do you wish that you could easily take the naive approach and assume that all people want good things for themselves rather than making inaccurate or negative assumptions?

Your dreams can come true

for the low, low cost of $9.99 plus S/H.

One daily spritz of the incredible Naive Body Spray will have you assuming positive intentions from the people around you all day long! As a bonus, if you order now, we will include a second Naive Body Spray disguised as bathroom air freshener to help out your grumpy coworkers!

Don't delay act today by calling 1-800-SpritzMe!

Once established, trust requires intentional work to maintain. People's values can change over time, and in order to cultivate trusting relationships, we need to understand those changes. The same four things it takes to establish trust are needed to sustain it: showing that you value the person with specific compliments, understanding each other's values, being playful at times, and acting with integrity are all necessary for maintaining trusting relationships. There will be times when we flub up and hurt the other person (or vice versa), but those hurdles don't have to be insurmountable if we fess up, apologize, and work hard not to make the same mistake again.

Once established, trust requires intentional work to maintain.

After a few months, Allie and Tinisha had established a trusting relationship. They sought out each other for help with work, for wardrobe advice, and to laugh over their mistakes. Allie talked with Tinisha about how she was feeling about her coworkers, so they decided to be intentional about not excluding anyone from their conversations. This helped Allie start to form trusting relationships with other colleagues too. Occasionally, she would slip back into old, guarded behavior.

Those old habits threatened to rise up one morning while Allie was preparing for a meeting. It was the biggest meeting she had ever been responsible for leading, and she literally felt like throwing up. With the meeting just minutes away, she was practicing some breathing techniques when Tinisha lightly knocked on her open office door.

"Hey, Allie! I was just thinking about you and wanted to catch you before the meeting starts. You look nervous. Are you nervous?"

"Tinisha, thanks, but I can't talk right now," Allie replied as she slowly closed her office door. Tinisha stepped back, looking hurt.

"Are you really going to close the door on me?"

Allie said nothing as she looked down and continued to close the door.

Oh great, on top of these crazy nerves, now I've offended Tinisha, she thought. *Great job, Allie. Old habits die hard, eh? You don't need to fight every battle on your own anymore. You have friends you can trust. Tinisha was just trying to help.*

Allie opened the door again, looked to her left then right before she spotted her friend. "Hey, Tinisha! Thank you, my friend." Allie gave her a little smile and a wave as Tinisha turned around.

Tinisha smiled big, gave Allie a reassuring thumbs up, and continued her journey back to her office.

•   •   •

Allie could have gone back to Tinisha after her important meeting to thank her for stopping by and to apologize for closing the door on her. That would have been nearly as effective as Allie's smile, wave, and thank you. By acting so quickly, Allie helped Tinisha avoid hours of emotional struggle, wondering if Allie was upset with her and whether their relationship was permanently damaged.

The point is, we will make mistakes. We will snap at the people we care about. We will revert to old behaviors and react too quickly when we feel stressed or threatened. But even those slipups can serve and strengthen our relationships *if* when we fall, we FAWL: fess up, apologize, and work hard to learn from our mistakes.

F ess up

A pologize

W ork hard to

L earn from our mistakes

There Is No Neutral

When it comes to relationships, there is no neutral. It is scary to consider, but it is true: Everything we do and everything we say is either building up our relationships or breaking them down. When we are walking down the hall, we can smile and greet our colleagues, which will positively contribute to relationships. Or we can put our heads down and get lost in our own thoughts and completely ignore our colleagues, which will hurt our relationships. There is no in-between, there is no neutral. I try to smile and greet strangers as if they are friends, because why not? Let's use every opportunity to add value to someone's life, to brighten others' days, even if just in passing at the grocery store.

Everything we do and everything we say is either building up our relationships or breaking them down.

Serendipitous Lessons

- Establishing trust takes intentional effort.
- To cultivate trust, you have to communicate that you value the other person, get to know each other's values, and act with integrity.
- Being playful may not be a "must" for establishing trust, but it sure helps.
- Maintaining trusting relationships takes intentional effort (and a daily spritz of Naive Body Spray).
- Values change over time and to sustain trust, we have to understand each other's changing values.
- We will make mistakes, but they can actually help build trust rather than destroy it if when we fall, we FAWL—Fess Up, Apologize, and Work hard to Learn from our mistakes.
- Like Allie, we cannot change everything about ourselves overnight. Any big change can start with small steps, one after the other, leading to amazing things.
- There is no neutral in relationships. *Everything* we do either contributes to the relationship or hurts the relationship. There is no in-between.

#SerendipityEDU

Think of a relationship that you value. Which characteristics helped establish the trust in that relationship? How could you apply those characteristics to another relationship where you are working to establish trust?

Share your story at #SerendipityEDU

Chapter 11
Glasser's Behavior Car

Just as your car runs more smoothly and requires less energy to go faster and farther when the wheels are in perfect alignment, you perform better when your thoughts, feelings, emotions, goals, and values are in balance.

—Brian Tracy

All behavior is driven by the five basic needs Dr. Glasser identified. Notice that I didn't say *wants*, but *needs*. We don't just want power, freedom, belonging, fun, and survival; we have an intrinsic need for them. If one of our tanks is running low, we will pull from our playbook of behaviors to find a behavior we have used before to meet that need. Being respectful means that even as we work to meet our needs, we don't prevent or interfere with others meeting their needs. An even higher goal is to meet our own needs while establishing and maintaining trusting relationships with the people around us.

To better understand ourselves and those around us, let's take our learning about William Glasser's Choice Theory even further. We know what drives our behavior, and we know we want to feel in effective control of our lives. But how do we do that when we are feeling frustrated, stressed out, overwhelmed, or furious? We cannot just snap our fingers and feel better. Sometimes we feel so badly that we can't think rationally.

We do *not* have direct control over our feelings. We *do*, however, have direct control over what we do physically. Right now, at this very moment, I am writing. I snuck off to my friend's cottage for a few hours of writing, and I feel a bit of pressure to make good use of this time away from my family. If I start to get anxious or stuck, I have some choices. I could stare at the computer screen. I could go grab a snack. I could take a walk out by the water. I could check my email. I could move on to another section of the book. I could reread what I have already written. Now that I think of it, I have lots of choices. Which one of those choices might help me change how I am feeling? Probably any of them other than the "stare at the screen" choice.

Dr. Glasser described our behavior with a car analogy. There are four wheels on a car, and they represent the four components of total behavior. The front wheels represent acting and thinking. The back wheels represent our emotional feelings and physiology. It is a front-wheel drive car, which means that our acting and thinking pull our emotions and our physiology along. In other words, what we do and how we think determine how we feel both emotionally and physically.

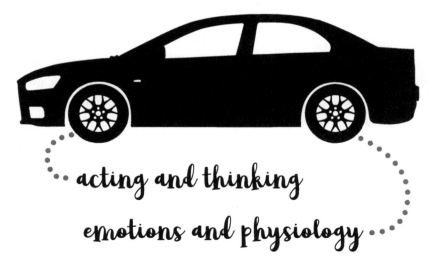

acting and thinking

emotions and physiology

When I am feeling anxious about my writing and I want to feel better and in more effective control, I can change what I am physically doing or how I am thinking. It is easiest to change our actions; sometimes it feels impossible to stop the thoughts that are going through our head.

Staring at the screen when I am anxious or at a loss for words is equivalent to taking no action at all, which will not help me feel better. Rereading what I've already written or going for a walk would be much better choices, because as soon as I change what I am doing, typically my thoughts change. By steering my acting and thinking in a different direction, my emotions and physiology follow along.

> By steering my acting and thinking in a different direction, my emotions and physiology follow along.

The idea that our emotions and physiology are greatly influenced by our thoughts and behavior is in line with *New York Times* bestselling author Gretchen Rubin's "one-minute rule."

> It's very simple: I must do any task that can be finished in one minute. Hang up my coat, read a letter and toss it, fill in a form, answer an email, note down a citation, pick up my phone messages, file a paper, put a dish in the dishwasher, replenish the diaper supply by the changing table, put the magazines away...and so on.
>
> Because the tasks are so quick, it isn't too hard to make myself follow the rule—but it has big results. **Keeping all those small, nagging tasks under control makes me more serene, less overwhelmed.**

Let's consider that idea in light of Dr. Glasser's behavior car. If you quickly accomplish that task you were thinking of, you are changing what you are doing and thinking from feeling overwhelmed by the number of things you have to do that day to feeling like you already got a start on your lengthy list of tasks. By changing to what you are doing and what you are thinking, you can help yourself feel better and even release that knot in your stomach or the headache that was developing.

When struggling students visit my office, they may need a few minutes to settle down. Many can do this on their own, but when a student is having a hard time regulating their emotions or they have experienced some sort of trauma in their lives, the emotional part of their brain (the limbic system or downstairs brain) may be driving their car. Getting them to do something—almost anything—is very helpful. They might want to write their feelings down, draw a picture, or work on a puzzle. If I start demanding things of them when their emotions are running on high, they likely will get even more elevated. Students cannot learn or work through problems when they are elevated emotionally. This is not just true for children; it is true for adults as well. As we know from Glasser's behavior car, we have the most direct control over our behavior. If we can guide students to do an activity that will help them think differently, they will begin to feel differently. Even five minutes of a calming activity can help a student (or really anyone) gain better control of their emotions and get ready for the next step.

How does understanding Dr. Glasser's behavior car this help us HANDLE each other with care? Understanding the behavior car and how to begin to change how we feel helps us be open to hope, helps us feel safe, helps us refrain from judgement, helps us think differently, helps us listen, and supports trusting relationships. When I am feeling wound up tighter than a ball of yarn, I know that going for walk or listening to music or a podcast for bit before I begin to process my feelings will be a great help. When I get to a calmer state, I'm better able to "peel the onion" of my emotions and get to the root of my bad feelings. The key to getting to this point of readiness for processing is the walk and the distraction. Here's a recent example: Someone said something hurtful to me about my lack of domestic skills. Tears instantly sprung to my eyes. I quickly got up from my chair and walked away. At first, I thought I might even have to get in my car and leave because I felt so hurt. I was totally stuck in my downstairs brain. But when I started walking, it took no more than fifty steps for me to calm my emotions, access my upstairs brain, and think more clearly. When I went back, I worked through the problem in a much more effective way than I would have before the walk.

I often wish for a "note to self" sticky note that I could constantly have with me to remind myself to not do anything until I am in control of my emotions. I can chalk up so many of the mistakes I have made to acting on emotions rather than making clear, intentional decisions.

Please excuse this commercial interruption . . .

Note-to-Self
Slap Bracelet

Ever have one of those no good, terrible days? One of those days when the monsters of self-doubt and fear in your head seem to be confirmed by the real-life events of the day?

One of those days where the positives and blessings of the previous days were washed away by the negative thoughts that take over your mind?

One of those days where you know you are drowning and you know you can save yourself, but you just can't figure out how?

Yup, we have all had awful days like that.

We all have days where it is best you zip your lips and postpone respond-ing to any emails for fear that you will take out your bad day on someone else. But, never again do we have to wake up the morning after one of "those days" feeling even worse because we regret all the nasty things we did while we were in a horrible mood. All we need is the handy-dandy...

Note-to-Self Slap Bracelet!

Not only is it super functional, it is beautiful too! Write your little note to yourself on the erasable bracelet, slap the bracelet on your wrist, and *presto!* You will wear your reminder all day long. I write, "Don't do it" on my bracelet when I am having a bad day to remind myself not to take my bad day out on others. If I need an extra reminder, I just take the bracelet off and slap it back on my wrist. It stings a little, but you can bet I don't press "send" on that sarcastic email.

You can even use the bracelet when you are having a good day as a reminder to "Be grateful." As a bonus, if you act now, a special marker and eraser will be included.

Don't delay! Get your Note-to-Self Slap Bracelet today for only $9.99 plus S/H!

There we go, exactly what I have been looking for! I will be ordering a few of those bracelets for myself and a few to give as gifts.

Serendipitous Lessons

- We have the most direct control over what we are physically doing.
- When we change what we are doing, we change what we are thinking.
- When we change our thinking, we often change how we are feeling, both emotionally and physically.
- Glasser's behavior car analogy helps us HANDLE each other with care because we know that in order to help someone feel better, they often need to change what they are doing first.
- A walk can clear the mind and solve so many problems.
- The Note-to-Self Slap Bracelet will sting less than the pain we feel after pressing "send" on a nasty email.

#SerendipityEDU

What is something you do that almost instantly helps you feel better? What connections did you make to Dr. Glasser's behavior car?

Share your story at #SerendipityEDU

Chapter 12

We All See the World Differently

Each person does see the world in a different way. There is not a single, unifying, objective truth. We're all limited by our perspective.

—Siri Hustvedt

Anger isn't just anger; it is so much more.
Anger deflects.
It covers up.
It blames.
It distracts.
It grabs attention.

When I was listening to Brené Brown's book *Daring Greatly* recently, I had to pause and reflect as she talked about anger being a socially acceptable cover-up emotion. I have to admit, anger baffles me. Of course, I do experience anger once in a while. Like after I ask my son for the hundredth time to do something as simple as pick up his socks and *he still hasn't done it.* Yeah, I get angry then. But what baffles me is the frequent anger I see in our world. And then Brown once again opened these foolish, foolish eyes. Anger isn't just anger. It is so much more.

When a young dad walks up to a salesperson at a grocery store and asks if there are any cans of formula in the back and is told no, it isn't socially acceptable for him to break down and weep even though that would reveal his true emotions. It is acceptable for him to fume and bark back at the salesperson and then stomp out of the store. This young dad is tired and desperate and doesn't want to disappoint his exhausted wife or his hungry child.

I am a school principal, so I am in a position to see anger used as a cover-up emotion on a regular basis. Anger rears its sometimes ugly head when children are insecure, when they are confused, or when they are scared. By talking with children, we can help them to identify what they are really feeling and to come up with strategies to help them work through those feelings. With adults, we often don't have the luxury to work through their underlying emotions with them. We just think they are jerks.

Brown's words in *Daring Greatly* prompted me to write these simple strategies to use when facing an angry person, or even when anger bubbles inside of us.

- **Understand that there is always more to the story.** People who are feeling great about themselves do not get steaming mad over someone cutting them off in traffic. There is something else going on there.
- **Give grace. Don't judge.** Judgement fuels anger. And it's not your job. You are not the judge and jury for every angry person out there. Neither am I. I have to remind myself of this frequently. Because, like I said, anger baffles me.
- **Do not personalize anger.** Even if it appears that way, ninety-nine percent of the time, their anger is not about you. It is about what is going on inside them. If you need

to, buy a pair of the Magic Mind-Reader Glasses to prove it to yourself.

As I see people getting angry over things that just happen in life and will always happen, like traffic, red lights, mistakes, or bad weather, I often think of my favorite quote of all time. Roman emperor Marcus Aurelius explained my conundrum with anger so eloquently. Join me in not worrying about those bitter cucumbers or briars in our path. They will always be there, and there are so many more things to concern ourselves about.

> *Is your cucumber bitter? Throw it away. Are there briars in your path? Turn aside. That is enough. Do not go on to say, "Why were things of this sort ever brought into the world?"*
>
> *—Marcus Aurelius*

We All Have Weak Spots

Everything we have experienced colors our world differently. Not only do we see things differently, we *feel* things differently. Something that may feel like a kind gesture to me may feel like a personal attack to someone else. A neighbor may do some lawn trimming for you, and in his mind he is generously helping you; he has the trimmer out, he is not in a hurry, and he knows you are busy. You look out and see him trimming your lawn and angrily think, *Seriously?!? He can't wait another day for me to get a chance to do it? He has to do it himself?* Another person may look out and think, *Oh my goodness, what a wonderful neighbor! I don't know when I would be able to get to the trimming.* The way we perceive others' behavior largely depends on our past experiences and our values. Our weak spots also color our perceptions.

Our weak spots are things that may or may not be true but that we fear about ourselves. When someone pokes a weak spot, it hurts—really badly. The person who became defensive about his neighbor trimming his lawn may be concerned with others thinking of him as lazy or disorganized. The dad who yells at the grocery store clerk for being out of formula may fear that people will think he isn't a good provider for his family.

> ## Our weak spots are things that may or may not be true but that we fear about ourselves.

Like everyone, I have a few weak spots. One is about my skills, or lack thereof, as a wife and mother. I am so not domestic. I can clean and organize, and I am an okay decorator, but that is the extent of my housewife-y skills. Now, to my credit, I have never actually been a housewife. I have always been a working mom. And I can remind myself of that until the cows come home, but my heart still harbors the feeling that I'm a bit of a failure because I don't bake, or cook delicious dinners, or clip coupons, or sew.

If someone's comments hit that particular weak spot of mine, if I don't pause to think first, I may react irrationally. A colleague might, for instance, start talking about her favorite dinner recipes and the rave reviews she gets from her family when she makes them. My gut reaction is to withdraw. Twinges of jealous and inadequacy arise in my heart. And even if her comments had nothing at all to do with me,

I may perceive them as criticism. It's irrational, I know. But that's what our weak spots can do.

Have you ever been around someone who suddenly becomes defensive about a topic that had nothing to do with him or her? Well, unbeknownst to you, you were likely talking about something that hit a weak spot.

When we become aware of our own weak spots as well as those of the people we love, we become better equipped to maintain strong, positive relationships. Understanding that we *all* have weak spots helps us respond kindly to what we perceive as irrational behavior or reactions from others. And becoming self-aware means we don't have to give in to our weak spots. That insight empowers us to do something about them.

Sometimes our weak spots are figments of our imaginations, and sometimes they are actual weaknesses, so first we need to do some reflection. When I sit down and think about my lack of domestic skills, if I first list all the things I do for my family, it helps me put my feelings of inadequacy into to perspective. I do a lot—both at home and at work. The fears I have about not being a domestic goddess are, at least in some areas, completely unfounded. But that reflection also helps me see areas where I can take steps to improve my skills, like trying a new recipe for dinner for my family once a week. Simple, intentional actions make me feel better about myself and act as a balm on that weak spot. It's Glasser's behavior car in action: changing what we are physically doing changes our thinking and pulls along our emotions.

Pros can Be Cons Too

Do you have that one friend who is always laughing and is incredibly uplifting? That one person in your life you are guaranteed to have a good time around? The one who feels really big positive emotions?

Does that same friend get really upset sometimes? Like, over the top and a little irrational kind of mad? So, here's the thing. Your friend feels in a big way. She feels big positive emotions, which is makes her super fun to be around when she is feeling good. But people who feel big positive emotions usually also feel big negative emotions. And when they are feeling negative, they are not nearly as fun to be around. But we don't get one side without the other.

Do you have another friend or family member who is really sensitive? He always seems to know just how you are feeling and knows the right thing to say. He feels with you. But if you ever tease him, he gets all bent out of shape. He is just as sensitive about himself as he is about you, and it may feel like he is overly sensitive about himself. That great quality of being super sensitive has pros and cons.

How about that detail-oriented person who is great at planning events because she plans everything down to the way the napkins are folded? You never have to worry about something falling through the cracks because she knows everything about everything and everyone. Then, do you sometimes get annoyed because she asks questions about things that aren't her business? Yup. I think you are getting the picture. That great detail-oriented person is not just detailed-oriented about the stuff you want her to be detail-oriented about. She is detail-oriented about *everything*. Even when you wish she wasn't.

Here's the really bad news. This reality is true about you too. The great traits that you have also have a downside. That is okay. Understanding this about ourselves helps us learn and grow. Understanding this about others allows us to give them grace and take the good with the bad, because we really can't have one without the other.

We All Have a Unique Lens

I don't think we can remind ourselves enough that we all see the world through a unique lens. Even shared experiences are viewed differently by two people sitting side by side. Sometimes the differences are extreme and sometimes the differences are pretty inconsequential, but they are always there. Recognizing the fact that we all see the world differently is so important to understanding others' behavior. It empowers us to give each other grace and to be empathetic. Understanding that we all look at the world through a unique lens also helps us remember that how others feel often has nothing to do with us. Let's look at some scenarios that highlight some common misconceptions we have about each other.

"I can't believe she would get so mad about that. I would never get mad about that."

It's true; you probably wouldn't. Unless you have been through all the same things she has been through. Then maybe you would. When someone seems to get mad at something you think is inconsequential, remind yourself how life experiences color what you see and how you feel. The same is true for everyone else. The reality is, the situation she is upset about has nothing to do with you. If you had lived through all the same things she has, you might get mad at whatever it is that seems silly to you now.

"Why is he always so cheerful? He must've never experienced anything bad in his life. I wish I could live an easy life like that. I'd be cheerful all the time too."

Nope. An easy life free from trouble or challenges doesn't exist. Everyone fights battles and goes through difficult times. There could be a myriad of reasons that someone chooses to have a cheery disposition almost all of the time. The person could be very selfless, and doesn't want to take his struggles out on others so he has practiced being cheerful over the years, and now it is his norm. The person might have a high need for fun, and it is much easier to be playful and laugh lots when he is cheerful. Or the person may be choosing a cheery disposition as a means of self-preservation. You know that saying, "If I don't laugh, I am going to cry. So I choose to laugh." Cheerfulness can also be a defense mechanism for the person who has a high need for power; letting others know that he is struggling with feelings is disempowering to him.

"She said, 'Have a nice day!' and I don't know what she means by that. Does she mean, 'Don't talk to me the rest of the day?' or is she really wishing me a nice day? I never know how to take her."

It is so hard to know how to interpret what someone means when they are often passive-aggressive. Even the nicest statements can be eyed warily and leave you wondering if they carry a nasty hidden meaning. It can be hard to understand why someone would choose to be passive-aggressive, so let's think in terms of Glasser's five basic needs. Which needs might be highest for someone who is passive-aggressive? Maybe he/she has high needs for both belonging and power. I imagine that it is very empowering to make passive-aggressive statements. It may feel like a way to meet the power need without direct confrontation, which someone who has a high need for belonging may avoid.

One of the best ways to deal with passive-aggressive behavior is to refuse to speak that language and assume positive intent. If someone says something that I think might be passive-aggressive, I say to myself, "Well, I don't speak passive-aggressive, so I will just have to take what they say at face value." If we take that approach, the passive-aggressive person might just stop using that tactic with you because it isn't need satisfying for them.

"He never talks to any of us. He must think that he is too good for us. Even when I ask him a question, he answers quickly and doesn't look at me. He is so stuck up."

I suppose there are people out there who are so full of themselves that they are very selective about whom they engage with. But there are other reasons people choose to be quiet and withdrawn—reasons that have nothing to do with you. The person you perceive as "stuck up" may have had a traumatic childhood during which the best way to avoid trouble was to be as quiet as possible and avoid eye contact. He may be second-guessing himself constantly in his mind and have very little self-confidence. It is ironic that being quiet can come across as arrogance when sometimes it is just the opposite.

"She is always teasing me. I mean, we don't even talk much so I don't know why she thinks that teasing me is a good idea. I am sick of it."

Teasing is one of those things that can help build relationships through fun and play. It can also create hard feelings and even destroy relationships. People typically tease each other to try to build a relationship. If someone is playfully teasing you, it may mean that they want to have a relationship with you where you know each other well enough to tease each other.

When I was a junior high teacher, we would have "family meetings" every day where we would build relationships, problem-solve, or just be curious together. We would dive into teasing every year in at least one family meeting, trying to decide if teasing is a good thing or a bad thing. In the end, we always came to the conclusion that it could be either, but that we have to be very careful with teasing. Before you tease someone, it is important to make sure you have a strong, positive relationship. Even with a strong relationship, we decided that we have to be very careful not to tease people about their weak spots. Which meant we had to know one another well enough to *know* those weak spots.

Let's visit Allie one last time to see how Tinisha felt after Allie snapped at her. Remember, Tinisha stopped by Allie's office to check on her before her big meeting.

• • •

After giving Allie the reassuring thumbs up, Tinisha continued on to her office, shaking her head as she thought to herself, *When are you going to learn that the world does not revolve around you? Allie's behavior had nothing to do with you, you dummy. She was nervous and her tank of emotions was about to overflow. Someday you will learn to stop taking personal offense at things that really have nothing to do with you.*

Tinisha thought back to how she had greeted Allie. *Oh man, I shouldn't have started that conversation by pointing out that Allie looked nervous. No wonder she snapped at me. I would have slammed the door in my face! Next time, when one of my friends looks like they are going to throw up because of their emotions, I will just encourage them. Live and learn, always.*

• • •

Tinisha recognized that Allie looks at the world through a different lens. She did not try to put herself in Allie's shoes. She did not think to herself, *Well, if a friend was coming to see me before a big meeting, I would at least thank them.* She accepted Allie and assumed positive intentions, and she practiced reflection to improve the way she supports those she cares about. I have some Tinishas in my life, and I am eternally grateful for them. And I want to be their Tinisha. Just like Tinisha, I am a constant work in progress.

When Self-Help Is Not Enough Help

As a pretty strong-willed person, I have learned to work my way through most of life's challenges. It takes time, it takes talking things through with people I love, it takes some difficult self-evaluation, and it takes seeking resources to help. Usually, though, I can work things out and move on. But not always.

There was a situation a few years back that I couldn't work through on my own. I am not afraid to ask for help when I need it, and in this particular situation, I needed help. I sought out a professional counselor, even though I considered myself a mature woman who should have been able to sort things out on her own (Whoops! I just shoulda'd on myself! Work in progress, always!), I knew I needed help. The counselor I spoke with helped me look at my situation through a different lens, which opened my eyes to new ideas and perspectives. In the end, I was mad at myself for not seeking help sooner.

I was able to work through my problems with my counselor and move on. Not everyone is so fortunate. Mental illness is a real thing that many people struggle with in the United States and throughout the world. I am not an expert in mental health, but I have seen family and friends battle mental health illnesses, and it is a battle that cannot be won alone.

This book is about helping others discover the best in themselves. Whether we're supporting people who have experienced trauma, drama, or mental illness, being able to understand another's perspective is essential to relating to them in a healthy and helpful way.

Help Is Available

Seeking help for a possible mental illness is one of the bravest things we can do. If you are suffering but unsure where to get help, your family doctor can be a great resource. In addition, there are many helplines you can call, text, or email. Here is the number to the National Alliance on Mental Illness: 1-800-950-NAMI (6264) or info@nami.org, which can be reached Monday through Friday, 10AM–6PM, ET.

If you or someone you know is ever feeling suicidal, please call 911 or you can contact the National Suicide Prevention Lifeline at 1-800-273-TALK (8255).

Serendipitous Lessons

- Anger is so much more than anger.
- We all have weak spots, and understanding our own weak spots and others' can help us better understand seemingly irrational reactions.
- All of our positive character traits have a downside. Recognize yours so you can learn and grow. Recognize others' so you can give them grace.
- We each view every situation we encounter differently, through our own lens of previous experiences and values.
- Sometimes self-help is not enough help. Seeking help for a possible mental illness is one of the bravest things we can do.
- I really do stink at cooking and most domestic things. On the upside, I can clean a kitchen like a boss!

#SerendipityEDU

What are your weak spots? How does knowing that help you understand your own behavior? Think of someone you love. What are his/her weak spots, and how does that help you better understand his/her behavior?

Share your story at #SerendipityEDU

Chapter 13

When We HANDLE Others with Care, It Takes a Toll

If your compassion does not include yourself, it is incomplete.

—Jack Kornfield

Have you ever heard the saying, "Misery loves company"? I think we can agree that adage is true on a few levels. First, if we are feeling miserable, we feel better knowing that we are not the only ones. When we learn that someone has the same gripe we do, we think, *Oh, thank goodness it is not only me. It must be their problem, not mine.*

"Misery loves company," is true in another way as well. When someone walks around with their head hanging low, moving slowly, and sighing often, what happens? People rush to them to see what is wrong. It is like asking for help without asking, it and can be very need-satisfying behavior. By acting sad, our need for belonging is met by those who rush to our aide. We could even meet our need for power that way because we often bring others down with us when we mope around.

So what is the opposite of "Misery loves company"? Is it "Happiness can be lonely"? In some ways, yes. I remember a time when a colleague and I were dealing with a tough situation. I tried to handle things without taking my frustration out on the people around me. I had a few people to talk the problem through with, but other than that, I carried on as normal and tried to support the people around me in the same way I always did.

My colleague handled the situation very differently, talking about it to practically everyone, crying frequently, and not making eye contact with others in the hallways. You can imagine that people treated us differently in response to our behavior. No one even mentioned the problem to me, while my colleague got hugs and sympathy galore. Carrying on in my typically happy state may have been helpful to the culture of our work environment and to my colleagues' well-being, but it was pretty lonely for me.

In addition, when you are in effective control of your life, enjoying almost every minute, and a happy affect is your norm, people bring you their problems. I know that many of the people who are reading this book are helpers; you seek out ways to help the people you care about. So, let's do the math…

Your own problems
+ the problems people bring you
+ the problems you find as a helper
= LOTS of problems

Have you ever seen one of those jugglers trying to balance a bunch of plates high above their heads on sticks? If you are a helper, you may feel just like that plate-spinning juggler at times. It can feel so rewarding to help others, and it can be absolutely exhausting at times—physically and emotionally. Even if we, as helpers, try not to take on the emotions of others, we are empathetic, so we feel *with* the people we care about.

Matters intensify when we are trying to help people who are struggling to regulate their own emotions. With these people, nothing is predictable. No wonder we collapse on the couch at the end of the day.

Caring for others leads to compassion fatigue because we can't simply switch off our empathy. It can also lead to vicarious or secondary trauma. Charles Figley, PhD, is a professor at Tulane University and director of Tulane's Traumatology Institute, and his quote sums up this idea perfectly.

> We have not been directly exposed to the trauma scene, but we hear the story told with such intensity, or we hear similar stories so often, or we have the gift and curse of extreme empathy and we suffer. We feel the feelings of our clients. We experience their fears. We dream their dreams. Eventually, we lose a certain spark of optimism, humor and hope. We tire. We aren't sick, but we aren't ourselves.

Awareness, however, is the first step to recovery. It is important to accept and understand that being compassionate to all and HANDLE-ing each other with care will take a toll on us, even the strongest of the strong will suffer with the people they are trying to help. That means that to help others, we have to take care of ourselves. We have to HANDLE ourselves with care first. All of the same principles that apply to being a trauma-informed and compassionate person apply to us.

Here are questions we can ask ourselves to HANDLE ourselves with care. These are great questions to ask yourself as you process through negative feelings. If you don't love talking to yourself, you could recruit a trusted friend to ask you these questions. They also work well when someone asks you for your help when they are working through a problem.

Hope Is Everything

Just a little spark of hope can reignite the fire within us. Spark hope with these questions:

- Can you remember a time when it was better?
- What is one thing you are thankful for right now?
- When you picture yourself in two weeks (two months, two years, etc.), what do you hope that picture looks like?
- Who helps you feel better in times like these? What might give you hope right now?
- What can you do right now that would help you feel better? Clean your closet? Dance like nobody's watching? Go see a movie? Exercise?

Assure Safety

Knowing that we are physically safe allows us to let down our guard and keep the problem in perspective. Use these questions to assure safety:

- What are you scared of right now?
- Are you in physical danger?
- Picture the worst thing that could happen and how you would handle that.
- Who helps you feel safe?

- What is something routine and normal that you could do right now?

No Shoulda' Needed

We are often our own worst enemy. It is just as important not to shoulda' on yourself as it is to not shoulda' on anyone else. Use these questions to avoid harsh self-judgement:

- You did the best you could at the time. What did you learn that would influence your reaction next time?
- You are enough. All you can do is move inch by inch toward the person you want to become. What goal do you have for yourself tomorrow?
- You are a gift to the world. What personal trait are you most proud of?

Do Things Differently

To get different results, we have to be different. This applies to how we treat ourselves also. If we want to feel different, we have to behave differently. Here are a few questions to help you be different:

- What do you want to change about how you feel right now? What could you do differently to support this change?
- What is within your control and what is not?
- What helped you the last time you were feeling this way?
- What didn't work the last time you were feeling this way?
- Think of someone you admire. What could you learn from how they handle situations like this?

Listen to Understand

It is important to take time to first validate your own feelings. You have a right to feel the way you do. Listening to our own heart is an important part of HANDLE-ing ourselves with care. Ask these questions and listen to yourself:

- Peel the onion down to its core to identify which problem is causing that sinking feeling in the pit of your stomach. What do you find there?
- What is the thing that weighs heaviest on your mind? How are you feeling about that?
- If you had right in your hands the thing you want most, what would it be?
- Who might help you process your feelings? Who do you turn to in times like these?

Establish Trust

So often we neglect to do for ourselves what we do for others. Trusting in the person we are and the person we are moving toward becoming is too important to neglect. Ask these questions to help establish trust in yourself:

- What do you love about yourself?
- What do you see in yourself that you would like to see in everyone else?
- Why do others trust you?
- Which trustworthy traits do you have, and how can they help you right now?

Living an effective life in a contented state does not mean that we don't need help and empathy from time to time. We do need help, and we don't often behave in a way that is asking for help without asking, so we actually have to ask. This is a great time to make a list of people you trust to help you process your feelings or work through a problem. It is okay if your list is short, because all we really need is one strong, positive relationship to pull us through the rough times.

Asking for help is human, and being humans together is important to maintaining trust. We don't want to put out a fake persona of being superhuman, someone who can tackle any problem with a flash of his pearly white smile and who never lets anything get him down. That type of person doesn't even exist in fairy tales. People don't trust infallible people because deep down, we know they don't exist, and we fear their judgement. Ask for help, share your struggles in a way that doesn't bring others down with you, and don't be afraid of your imperfect humanness. It is a gift.

> ## Don't be afraid of your imperfect humanness. It is a gift.

When to Let Go

The people we surround ourselves with either raise or lower our standards. They either help us to become the best version of ourselves or encourage us to become lesser versions of ourselves. We become like our friends. No man becomes great on his own. No woman becomes great on her own. The people around them help to make them great.

We all need people in our lives who raise our standards, remind us of our essential purpose, and challenge us to become the best version of ourselves.

—Matthew Kelly

It is so very true that we are who we surround ourselves with, and as caring, loving people, we may have great difficulty letting someone go from our lives. It may feel like quitting, and it may break our hearts, but, in order to take care of ourselves, we may have to let go sometimes. We were meant to fly, and if we have people in our lives constantly trying to clip our wings, we are not being true to ourselves, and we are not living our best lives. We may have to let someone go completely, or we may be able to lessen their influence and involvement in our lives. The bottom line is that not only is it okay, it is sometimes absolutely necessary to let go.

Serendipitous Lessons

- Happiness can be lonely unless we ask for help when we need it.
- Trying to balance your own problems and others' problems can lead to compassion fatigue and secondary trauma.
- It is just as important to HANDLE ourselves with care as it is to HANDLE others with care.
- We all need help from time to time, even the helpers.
- Being human and exposing flaws and vulnerability can help not only ourselves but can help others work through their own flaws and can help keep trust in our relationships.
- If someone in your life is trying to clip your wings, you may have to let them go, even if it breaks your heart.

#SerendipityEDU

When looking at yourself with the same compassion that you afford others, what reflections did you have? Which questions hit home for you? What questions would you add to this list?

Share your story at #SerendipityEDU

Chapter 14
The Journey Continues

*Pursue some path, however narrow
and crooked, in which you can walk
with love and reverence.*

—Henry David Thoreau

One day, a young man visited my office. He wanted to share a concern with me. He felt like he was being mistreated by a classmate and wanted my help. I looked into his eyes, and I thought, *If not me, then who?* This little boy's parents did not speak English, and they could not advocate for him in the same way other parents advocated for their children. If I didn't advocate for him, then who would?

A friend was struggling to solve a problem and wanted my help. The problem was relatively urgent, so she needed to talk it over right then. I looked around at all the work I expected to accomplish in the short time I had available that day. I did not have the time to give her but decided to make the time. Because if not me, then who?

A person reached out to me on Twitter about a connection he made to my book *The Path to Serendipity* and wanted some guidance. I first asked some questions and then shared my understanding of his situation to make sure I was interpreting him accurately. Then I suggested some things for him to think about. I didn't know him and had no obligation to help him, but if not me, then who?

If not you, then who? If not now, then when?

The list of the challenges the people around us face are endless. Physical disabilities, discrimination, sickness, mental illnesses, history of trauma, current trauma, vicarious trauma, poverty, self-doubt, learning disabilities, developmental disabilities, and so much more. Or someone could be dedicating everything they have to lessen the impact of one of these challenges on a loved one. You guys, for real, life is so very, very hard. Life is beautiful in its complexity, and there is so much to learn on this roller coaster path our life takes us on. But we cannot deny the challenges we all face. We can, however, always HANDLE each other with care.

> Life is beautiful in its complexity, and there is so much to learn on this rollercoaster path our life takes us on.

Let's not just care for the people who seem to get punched with every challenge possible; let's also care for the people who never tell us about the challenges they face. Let's not only care for the person with the obvious physical disability; let's care for the person with the not-so-obvious mental illness, too. Every single person deserves our care, and they don't need our judgement.

When we started *Through the Lens of Serendipity*, we were looking to accomplish eight goals.

1. Know that there is always more to someone's story than what meets the eye.
2. Review (or learn about) Glasser's five basic needs and expand on that learning by understanding how to change how we are thinking and feeling.
3. Understand that looking for the good in all people benefits more than just the people around you. It benefits you as well.
4. Begin to understand how our brains work and why someone might choose fight, flight, or freeze over pausing and problem-solving.
5. Understand what trauma is and that the same compassion and supports that those who have been affected by trauma can benefit ALL people.
6. Know that others' past experiences change their view on the world and their perceptions of others, and motivate their own self-preserving behaviors. And our own past experiences change our view of the world.
7. Understand that we impact each other with our behavior, and this impact can be negative or positive.
8. Wholeheartedly believe that in order to support everyone, we have to HANDLE each other with care.

Now that we have accomplished these eight goals, are we ready to go out there and HANDLE each other with care? Are we ready to love and support everyone for everything they are?

Hope is everything: Hope is something we can freely give to others. It can be a smile at a stranger you pass in the street or a simple question about when times were better to a friend. Will you give hope to the hopeless?

Assure safety: Does your presence assure safety to those you love? Are you ready to support others in feeling safe within themselves?

no shoulda' needed: Will you avoid judgement and strip the word "should" from your vocabulary?

Do things differently: Do you accept that in order to get different results, you have to be different?

Listen: Might you listen to understand through the good times as well as the bad? We know we will never be able to be in their shoes with all their previous experiences, but are you ready to listen well enough to feel with them?

Establish trust: Can you communicate that you value others, communicate your own values, be playful, and act with integrity? Do you appreciate the importance of establishing trust, knowing that trust has to come first before a relationship can truly develop?

We can change the world, one interaction at a time. Share a smile, lighten the load of the people around you, change judgmental thoughts into hopeful curiosity, lend a hand. Do what we can with what we have, making sure that we prioritize taking care of ourselves. That is all. You are perfectly poised to handle everyone you meet with the same care you need. There is no better time than now, and if not you, then who?

#SerendipityEDU

Thank you so much for joining me on this journey. We are continuous works in progress, and we are better together. Please share your connections and your ideas using #SerendipityEDU as you embark on the next step of your path to helping others discover the best in themselves.

Don't try to change the world,
Find something that you love
And do it every day
Do that for the rest of your life
And eventually,
The world will change

—Macklemore

Resources

Brown, Brené. *Daring Greatly: How the Courage to Be Vulnerable Transforms the Way We Live, Love, Parent, and Lead*. New York: Avery, 2012.

Cherry, Kendra. "How the Availability Heuristic Affects Decision-Making." *Very Well Mind*. September 10, 2018. verywellmind.com/availability-heuristic-2794824.

Figley, PhD, Charles R., ed. *Compassion Fatigue: Secondary Traumatic Stress Disorders from Treating the Traumatized*. New York: Taylor & Francis Group, 1995.

Glasser, MD, William. *Choice Theory: A New Psychology of Personal Freedom*. New York: HarperPerennial, 1999.

Kelly, Matthew. *The Rhythm of Life: Living Every Day with Passion and Purpose*. New York: Beacon Publishing, 2004.

Osteen, Joel. "Pastor Joel Osteen's Full Sermon 'The Power of I Am' | Oprah's Life Class | Oprah Winfrey Network." YouTube Video 27:29. October 28, 2012. youtube.com/watch?v=_kjSK-PcU9o.

Rubin, Gretchen. "Need a Simple and Effective Way to Get Your Life Under Control? Try the 'One-Minute Rule.'" *Happier with Gretchen Rubin Podcast*. gretchenrubin.com/2006/12/need_a_simple_a/.

Siegel, MD, Daniel J. and Tina Payne Bryson, PhD. *The Whole-Brain Child: 12 Revolutionary Strategies to Nurture Your Child's Developing Mind*. New York: Bantam Books, 2011.

The Whole-Brain Child Workbook: Practical Exercises, Worksheets and Activities to Nurture Developing Minds. Eau Claire, WI: PESI Publishing & Media, 2015.

Supin, Jeanne. "The Long Shadow: Bruce Perry on the Lingering Effects of Childhood Trauma. *The Sun* (November 2016): 4–13. childtrauma.org/wp-content/uploads/2016/12/Sun-Interview-Bruce-Perry-Nov-2016.pdf.

With Gratitude

We get just one beautiful life, and I am so grateful that mine is filled with people who believe in me, who bring me great joy, who cry with me and laugh with me. People who open my eyes and open my heart and teach me valuable lessons. I pray that you know who you are, that I have expressed my gratitude and appreciation to all of you.

Thank you to my husband, Jim, for pretending to listen every single time I read my writing to you, and thank you for believing in me even when I didn't believe in myself. Thank you to my dad for always telling me that I should write a book. Thank you to George Couros, who inspired me to start this writing journey. Thank you to Dave and Shelley Burgess, for amplifying the voice of amazing educators and for taking a chance on me. Thank you to Erin Casey and her fantastic editing team for making my writing so much smarter. Thank you to Genesis Kohler for the beautiful cover design.

I am so very blessed.

Love always,

Allyson

Also from Allyson Apsey

The Path to Serendipity
Discover the Gifts along Life's Journey

The best gift life gives us is the freedom to choose who you want to be and what kind of life you want to live. In *The Path to Serendipity*, educational leader Allyson Apsey offers a funny, genuine, and clever look at the fortunes we can gain from even our worst experiences. Through her personal, relatable stories, you will learn strategies for living a meaningful life regardless of the craziness happening around you.

The Princes of Serendip

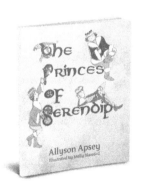

In *The Princes of Serendip*, Allyson Apsey offers a twist on an age-old tale and reveals the true meaning of the word serendipity. Join the three princes as they learn that hard work, love, and living life to its fullest just may be the path to discovering the greatest joys life has to offer.

#SerendipityEDU

Bring Through the Lens of Serendipity
to Your Organization or Event

Allyson is a dynamic national speaker who fills the room with energy. She specializes in captivating presentations that are emotional journeys for all present. The participants are laughing, crying, surprised, and reflecting throughout their time together. She often incorporates multimedia technology tools to support the interactive format. There is no doubt that participants walk out of her keynotes or presentations changed, with new perspectives, new goals, and strategies to implement right away.

Popular topics from Allyson Apsey:

- Helping Others Discover the Best in Themselves
- HANDLE-ing Each Other with Care
- Discovering the Path to Serendipity
- Leading from the Inside Out
- Creating Need-Satisfying Environments Where People Thrive
- Supporting Students, Staff, and Families Affected by Trauma
- Building Strong, Positive Relationships

Contact Allyson Apsey via email
at allysonapsey@gmail.com.

More from
Dave Burgess Consulting, Inc.

Since 2012, DBCI has been publishing books that inspire and equip educators to be their best. For more information on our DBCI titles or to purchase bulk orders for your school, district, or book study, visit **DaveBurgessConsulting.com/DBCBooks**.

More from the Like a *PIRATE*™ Series

Teach Like a PIRATE by Dave Burgess

Explore Like a Pirate by Michael Matera

Learn Like a Pirate by Paul Solarz

Play Like a Pirate by Quinn Rollins

Run Like a Pirate by Adam Welcome

Lead Like a PIRATE™ Series

Lead Like a PIRATE by Shelley Burgess and Beth Houf

Balance Like a Pirate by Jessica Cabeen, Jessica Johnson, and Sarah Johnson

Lead with Culture by Jay Billy

Lead with Literacy by Mandy Ellis

Lead beyond Your Title by Nili Bartley

Leadership & School Culture

Culturize by Jimmy Casas

Escaping the School Leader's Dunk Tank by Rebecca Coda and Rick Jetter

The Innovator's Mindset by George Couros

Kids Deserve It! by Todd Nesloney and Adam Welcome

Let Them Speak by Rebecca Coda and Rick

Start. Right. Now. by Todd Whitaker, Jeffrey Zoul, and Jimmy Casas

Stop. Right. Now. by Jimmy Casas and Jeffrey Zoul Jetter

The Limitless School by Abe Hege and Adam Dovico

The Pepper Effect by Sean Gaillard

The Principled Principal by Jeffrey Zoul and Anthony McConnell

The Secret Solution by Todd Whitaker, Sam Miller, and Ryan Donlan

They Call Me "Mr. De" by Frank DeAngelis

Unmapped Potential by Julie Hasson and Missy Lennard

Your School Rocks by Ryan McLane and Eric Lowe

Technology & Tools

50 Things You Can Do with Google Classroom by Alice Keeler and Libbi Miller

50 Things to Go Further with Google Classroom by Alice Keeler and Libbi Miller

140 Twitter Tips for Educators by Brad Currie, Billy Krakower, and Scott Rocco

Code Breaker by Brian Aspinall

Creatively Productive by Lisa Johnson

Google Apps for Littles by Christine Pinto and Alice Keeler

Master the Media by Julie Smith

Shake Up Learning by Kasey Bell

Social LEADia by Jennifer Casa-Todd

Teaching Math with Google Apps by Alice Keeler and
 Diana Herrington

Teaching Methods & Materials

All 4s and 5s by Andrew Sharos

Ditch That Homework by Matt Miller and Alice Keeler

Ditch That Textbook by Matt Miller

Educated by Design by Michael Cohen

The EduProtocol Field Guide by Marlena Hebern and
 Jon Corippo

Instant Relevance by Denis Sheeran

LAUNCH by John Spencer and A.J. Juliani

Make Learning MAGICAL by Tisha Richmond

Pure Genius by Don Wettrick

Shift This! by Joy Kirr

Spark Learning by Ramsey Musallam

Sparks in the Dark by Travis Crowder and Todd Nesloney

Table Talk Math by John Stevens

The Classroom Chef by John Stevens and Matt Vaudrey

The Wild Card by Hope and Wade King

The Writing on the Classroom Wall by Steve Wyborney

**Inspiration, Professional Growth,
& Personal Development**

The Four O'Clock Faculty by Rich Czyz

Be REAL by Tara Martin

Be the One for Kids by Ryan Sheehy

The EduNinja Mindset by Jennifer Burdis

How Much Water Do We Have? by Pete and Kris Nunweiler

P Is for Pirate by Dave and Shelley Burgess

The Path to Serendipity by Allyson Apsey

Sanctuaries by Dan Tricarico

Shattering the Perfect Teacher Myth by Aaron Hogan

Stories from Webb by Todd Nesloney

Talk to Me by Kim Bearden

The Zen Teacher by Dan Tricarico

Children's Books

Dolphins in Trees by Aaron Polansky

The Princes of Serendip by Allyson Apsey

About the Author

Allyson Apsey has been an educator for over twenty years; a school leader for fifteen of those years. She is passionate about students and staff and leads others through their strengths. She tries to be transparent, vulnerable, and supportive, and she doesn't ask questions unless she wants the answers.

Despite the fact that she never wanted to set foot in a school again after high school graduation, there is nowhere else she'd rather spend her days than in classrooms. In fact, she doesn't even have a chair at her desk because she is moving around the school all day long. The challenges and delights of being a principal fill her days with joy. Allyson enjoys nothing more than helping others be the very best they can be.

Allyson is so proud of her school district and the Zeeland, Michigan, community, and she loves being the principal of Quincy Elementary. She cannot image a more dedicated, passionate, and skilled group of teachers. They illicit wonder, excitement, and a love for learning in their students.

Recognizing the significant impact trauma has had on many of our students, staff, and families, Allyson completed a program to become a certified trauma practitioner in education. The supports students affected by trauma need are beneficial to all students because they are grounded in a foundational core of strong, positive relationships based on trust. Allyson is also certified in William Glasser's Choice Theory and reality therapy.

Allyson is honored to serve on the executive board of directors for MEMSPA (Michigan Elementary and Middle School Principals Association) as the State and Federal Relations Co-Coordinator. Additionally, she is on the steering committee for MACUL (Michigan Association for Computer Users in Learning) SIG-ADMIN. Allyson enjoys working with and learning from amazing educational leaders in both of these organizations.

Allyson writes on a blog called *Serendipity in Education*, and this is her third book. She is also the author of *The Path to Serendipity* and the picture book *The Princes of Serendip*, both published by Dave Burgess Consulting, Inc. Allyson also loves speaking to passionate groups of educators about working to be happy and effective people for the benefit of everyone around us.

Allyson is married to Jim, and she has two amazing sons with him: Laine and Tyson.

She is blessed.

Connect with Allyson. We are better together.

 *AllysonApsey.com*

 *allysonapsey@gmail.com*

 *@AllysonApsey*

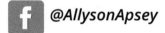 *@AllysonApsey*

CPSIA information can be obtained
at www.ICGtesting.com
Printed in the USA
FFHW012353180419
51829021-57233FF